THE GREATER GLORY

Jean Bacon

translated by Philip Bacon

PRISM
PRESS

BRIDPORT, DORSET · SAN LEANDRO, CALIFORNIA

This book is dedicated to
the hundreds of millions of dead
in wars past, present, and to come.

Published by PRISM PRESS, 1986
2 South Street, Bridport,
Dorset DT6 3NQ

and

PRISM PRESS
P.O. Box 778, San Leandro,
California 94577, USA

ISBN 0 907061 91 5

First published in France under the title
Les Saigneurs de la Guerre
by Editions Gallimard, Paris

© Les Presses d'Aujourd'hui, 1981

Typeset in Baskerville by Margaret Spooner Typesetting,
Bridport, Dorset
Printed by The Guernsey Press Ltd., Guernsey

Contents

Prologue

Together with eating and sex, warfare is man's most frequent occupation. Research has shown that if you take three thousand years of civilization and average them out, you get thirteen years of war for every one of peace. One can only pay silent tribute to such extraordinary determination. It is fitting confirmation, if any were needed, of the title earned by man —master of the world.

With very few exceptions, animals have no knowledge of the human pleasure of tearing each other to pieces in acts of fratricidal and collective war. In their stupid way, they are content to kill only animals of other species for food, as we do ourselves with the great piles of beasts which contribute unwillingly to our daily gorgings — every sort of animal, whether it flies, swims or walks.

More to the point, these inferior creatures have been given a natural instinct of inhibition which takes over if they find themselves confronting one of their own species. This cools them down and prevents their race from suffering ultimate extinction.

Thank God, man has for long dispensed with such feeble restrictions. Nothing bars his way on his murderous path. He wallows deliciously in the blood of his race. For centuries he has dreamt of ways of staging ever more impressive slaughters, delightedly taxing his intelligence as to how to find the best solution to the problem. His only thought is whether it is better to cut his enemy to pieces, burn him, suffocate him, blow him up or machine-gun him. He is drunk with the joy of his creative impulse. He has made such progress recently that he may even be able to achieve his final ambition — the obliteration of the world.

It is up to us not to be caught unawares, not to let slip an opportunity which may not occur again, with time running out. We must examine the fascinating phenomenon we call war — we will not regret it.

Chapter 1:
From Muscle-power to the Law

Cavemen made the early discovery that they possess bigger muscles than their female companions, and used their strength to strike terror into the hearts of women and children alike. The minute man becomes aware of another will resisting his own, he hits out. He thus establishes his right of supremacy in the family hierarchy. From that, flows the hierarchical structure of the tribe, then of the nation. These are merely natural consequences of the fundamental law that might is right.

The same goes for international law. Only superior force can resolve a dispute between two states — nothing will be gained by talks, negotiations or compromise solutions. The quality of nations can only be measured by war — by being put to the test in battle. War is the only reliable arbiter, ignoring privileges, ancient rights and legitimate claims alike. Allowing for no under-the-counter negotiations, bargaining or undue pressure of any sort, this relentless tribunal is the most elevated form of justice. War is "a legislation quite incorruptible, with no judge, no witness, no jury, no courtroom, whose findings have no right of appeal."[1]

A trial of strength, war arrives at a verdict by pointing out the winner, she puts right on his side. No further argument is possible, and an unequivocal statement has been made. Yesterday's rebels, who during the battle became the government-in-exile, then the provisional government, are today the legitimate power. Had they lost, they would have been shot. But they won; simply because they were on the right side, the stronger side, which is, of course, the better side. That is one of the wonderful things about the judgement of war: it gives victory to the most deserving country. The winner was meant to win. "Just as the most perfect of beings will win in man-to-man combat, so the most perfect of nations will triumph in an international struggle."[2] It may be argued that such a shining example of nationhood must enjoy the advantage of efficient weaponry, but — and here we must admire the reasoning of philosophers — these weapons were designed by the country's engineers, and built by their technicians and workmen, which makes them the product of the nation's genius. And even if they had to be bought overseas, the currency which pays for them comes from the nation's wealth — yet more evidence of the genius of men who produce wealth through ownership of oil, uranium or steel.

On the other hand, the loser is the one who deserved to lose, even if he was the victim of a treacherous attack, or if he was beaten by an alliance of several ambitious and unscrupulous states. Corruption, idleness and immorality are seen to be the cause of his defeat. Germany makes war on little Denmark and understandably crushes her; which goes to show that Danes are inferior in intelligence, bravery, loyalty and wisdom to Germans.

Does this mean we have to accept that chance plays no part in war? It would be against the doctrine of that great man Clausewitz, who gives chance an important place in the running of a battle. What, after all, is Chance, if not Providence, or Fortune? And everyone knows that Fortune smiles on the brave, in other words on the strong.

*   *   *

Man did not resort to the radical solution of war to resolve arguments, without first trying many alternatives.

Some people have thought of replacing war with a competitive sport, where the protagonists would be represented by champions. This is not a new idea, but one that has found favour many times in the past.

Serious drawbacks emerge, though. In a real battle, the few rules there are can be broken without trouble, since there is no judge or comeback. On the other hand, imagine a game where players ignore the referee's whistle and do what they want, irrespective of penalties, fouls, hand-ball or offside. What is more, it might seem odd if one team had three or four times as many players as the other, and if they won, their captain would almost certainly be booed. Nothing of the sort would occur in a military engagement. Any general who manages to acquire more tanks, planes and bombs than his enemy, who fights three against one and inevitably wins the day, is carried shoulder-high in triumphant celebration.

No-one will shout: unfair! You do nothing dishonourable in war, except if you lose.

Man has sought another alternative to war by instituting

long-term agreements for peace. There are so many it is not possible to examine them all. Besides, they make pathetic reading. It would appear that every hare-brained idealist, simpleton and builder of castles in Spain has given free reign to his appalling fantasies full of puerile ideas. The Kellog Treaty must be the jewel of the crown. Enough of war! War is banned! Almost as if one said Enough of whirlwinds! Earthquakes are banned!

This idea has spread. Proposals to outlaw warfare are beyond number, including those put forward right in the middle of the last world war. The concept was solemnly abolished on 16th August 1941 by the Atlantic Charter, on 21 September 1943 by the American House of Representatives, and the following month by the Moscow conference. To cap it all, it has even been abolished by servicemen. For instance, in a statement he made on 26th January 1955, General MacArthur, former commander-in-chief of the American forces in Korea, announced that the time had come to abolish war and proclaim it illegal. To which the famous British journalist James Cameron replied: "This has all the practical value of writing a no-measles clause into a baby's birth certificate."

* * *

It is important to pay attention to the homeopathic efforts to establish universal peace, by using evil to cure evil. We will wage war one last time to end it for good. That was the excuse of the Romans, of Charlemagne, of Napoleon, of the British, of Hitler, and of every conqueror. It is still the dream of the great powers, caring for us as they do, to present us with the Pax Americana, or the Pax Sovietica, as a prelude to the Pax Humana. Sad to say, it has never worked. The Pax Romana was a myth. As soon as the Macedonian Empire was destroyed, the conquering leaders remembered the maxim that God helps those who help themselves, raised armies of their own and fought bloody internecine wars. Charlemagne was barely cold in his grave when his heirs embarked on ferocious wars to divide up the succession. Pax Britannica is a fine example of English humour. During its time, there were countless expeditions of conquest against Burma, Egypt, Afghanistan, China, Mexico, against the Khefirs, Zulus and Boers. Hitler and Napoleon certainly attempted to establish their ideas of world peace, and if they failed so pitifully, it must be because it is more difficult than it seems to impose a new moral order, to establish an ideal of understanding, trust and brotherhood, through violence or destruction.

There is one other thing which realists never fail to point out to proponents of world government. They say that such a solution reveals an inherent weakness, quite apart from whatever practical difficulties might exist. It presupposes that from the great day of signing a universal charter, the world will stand still; inter-state relations will remain fixed, frontiers frozen. This is an incredible piece of reasoning. One might as well give up right away if supporters of world government are so stupid as to believe that relations between governments will never change and that the status quo will operate forever. In fact, these advocates of world government are not as idiotic as might be thought. They have suggested a system of arbitration responsible for any adjustments made necessary by the constant changes occurring in society. Unfortunately, nations which are quite happy to go to arbitration over seals in the Baring Straits or toxic fumes from a factory on a neighbouring coast, are not so pleased about dealing with political problems.

As everyone knows, the least dispute then becomes a question of life and death, and puts the very existence of the country into doubt. Come to think of it, it is very surprising that any single nation has managed to survive in this world, considering that every defeated state must inevitably have disappeared off the face of the earth.

Let us suppose that arbitration should be made compulsory — God forbid! How far back would we have to go to authenticate a claim? How many years, before how many wars? What claim do men of Norman descent have in England? Or does the legitimate claim belong to the Saxons before them? Or the Romans, who were there too? Or the early Britons? Or does one go all the way back to Neanderthal Man?

Great statesmen and diplomats have always known that politics and diplomacy are mobile social phenomena, and that promises are not worth the paper they are written on. Promises extracted by force are obviously worthless. As for those which have been made willingly, they do not need to be kept if they go against the interests of the state. Machiavelli wrote: "this is the correct point of view, and only if men were well disposed to one another would it not be so. Since men are evil and do not keep their word, why keep yours? In any event does a Prince not have perfectly fitting reasons for carrying out something other than what he promised?"

Politics is like love. Preaching about it means little. Nothing can illustrate this better than the peace treaty. Most treaties were formally agreed after careful thought and lengthy discussions which sometimes went on for several years. These treaties run to many pages and every possible eventuality has been taken into consideration most thoroughly. In them are touching expressions of undying friendship, and undertakings about new eras of peace and prosperity in a world free from threats and injustice at last.

But what is the true situation? The answer is to be found in statistics. Of the 8,400 treaties which are available for examination between the years 1500 BC and 1860 AD, the average lifespan of agreements amounts to two years, where they were meant to last forever. This is because the role of a peace treaty is to reinforce one country's victory and another's defeat, thus prolonging an extremely precarious state of affairs.

As soon as the situation changes, the treaty becomes worthless. It can barely commit a government let alone a country, and that for only a few months, let alone a few years. So much so that treaties often carry within them the seed of future conflict. Such was the case with the Treaty of Versailles, with its clause concerning the Danzig corridor or the restrictions over the Trieste region. Diplomats are too devious to destroy utterly the roots of ancient disputes. They know that war is necessary and they allow its fire to smoulder under the ashes.

Besides, how can we hope to bring together in a homogeneous whole the states which divide up the entire world? Too many differences exist between them, whether of race, religion, language or culture. Apart from the paltry detail that they are made up of human beings, they have nothing whatsoever in common.

But dreams die hard — especially the one of the world's nations brought together in one huge universal city under a single world government. Men like Dr. Hutchins, Chancellor of the University of Chicago, the English philosopher Bertrand Russell, or Pandit Nehru come back to such marginal and fantastic views. Luckily for us, this handful of isolated voices has no following. The vast majority of men thinks quite differently. And we are with them, since it is impossible that so many could be wrong — those who show us how to think, eminent people all — our superiors, whether they be politician, military chief, trade unionist, industrialist or civil servant. All back with an impressive unity the principle which makes redundant any attempt at effective cooperation between peoples — the principle of national sovereignty.

Every relevant speech, statement or article, whether it deals with the European Parliament, or the Middle or Far East, or the rights of man, uses in abundance those key words of modern diplomacy: independence, autonomy, freedom, non-interference.

This concept of national independence has had the most fortuitous effect on those devious efforts which have been made after conflicts have ceased. The total impotence of the League of Nations happened thanks to the thoughtful principle which allowed any of its members to withdraw when they wished, i.e. if a decision was going against them. Admire the logic of those who set up the machinery created to end war. The League of Nations had an inbuilt respect for state sovereignty, but states see as vital their right to make war. So the League supported this sacred right. One or two conditions were made, such as the need for a justifiable cause. Such treaties allowed both sides to possess armies, adequately equipped, to carry out manoeuvres, and even to go so far as to impose mobilisation which, as Raymond Poincaré said in 1914, is not a declaration of war, but which invariably precedes it very closely. A nation so doing is asked simply to begin by exhausting all peaceful means to a solution. The plaintiff appeals to the court, and takes the precaution of taking with him a dozen hand grenades in case the judge is unable to bring about a settlement. The final point to make is that major decisions have to be passed unanimously. This was the great invention of the League which was faithfully preserved by the United Nations through the right of veto. Let us see how this works.

As soon as a great power believes that a Security Council motion could be prejudicial to its interests, she vetoes it. In other words, she can be safely assured that nothing can ever be decided which goes against her ambitions, lessens her prestige, or prevents her territorial growth, all of which reflect tenets of nationalism. In theory, only smaller nations which do not benefit from the right of veto could find themselves forced into decisions against their interests. What happens in practice negates this injustice, as the little powers completely ignore UN motions which they consider detrimental.

This has happened with Israel, Nigeria, and Pakistan, in a long series of broken ceasefires and truces. Even Britain has successfully ignored UN resolutions concerning her dispute with Argentina. Another interesting characteristic of the United Nations organisation is that it allows and even recommends there should be alliances and treaties of friendship, non-aggression, mutual help and so on.

This would imply that the UN's guarantees are not foolproof, and that it is a good idea to back them up with extra ties, even though these may contradict the general principles of the UN charter. After all, one or other must be right: either the Charter is a serious undertaking which anticipates every possible area of conflict and seeks to arbitrate, which makes it needless or even damaging to add extra weight through secondary, perhaps contradictory agreements; or the charter is a simple and costly joke, which has to be made clear to the world.

We believe the second hypothesis to be the more likely.

Do away with the UN, and everything becomes clearer. No more misunderstandings. Everyone would then know that the world's nations are autonomous and independent, free to sort out their problems the way they want. They would get back their pride, and no-one would have to make concessions to keep the peace. Battles would rage at once, with complete honesty. Once the fighting had ended, it might well be that nations would see the justice of solutions which peacemakers had offered hesitantly, and which had been fiercely rejected as unacceptable for preserving the dignity of protagonists. This is under-standable, as laying countries waste, bloodbaths, millions of lives sacrificed, enable adversaries to regain their dignity. At that point, concessions can be made.

Such a concept of national sovereignty is universally accepted today, even by nations which an observer might think do not worry themselves about it overmuch given the circumstances. When armies of the Warsaw Pact invaded Czechoslovakia in 1968, there was no question of undue interference in the affairs of that country, even less of a violation of her sovereignty. Rather it was the act of the real friends of the Czech people, come to defend the integrity and independence of a sister nation. The Soviet government had remained faithful to the declaration made in 1962 when it accused Western powers of meddling in the affairs of the Congo. No nation or group of nations, ran that statement, should take such a risk as to control the fate of

overeign state. This golden rule has always been
, despite appearances. For proof, you need only look at
n intervention in Vietnam or Korea, Greeks and Turks
rus, French and Libyans in Chad, English in Aden,
Cubans in Angola, Vietnamese in Cambodia and Russians in
Afghanistan.

Chapter 2
The Scales and the Sword

In what circumstances can a war be said to be just? That question has always exercised our minds. The Romans did not bother to complicate matters. As far as they were concerned, a war was just if it had been declared according to the rules laid down. Special priests-cum-magistrates acted as ambassadors to the offending — or allegedly offending — nation. They would explain in detail Rome's grievances, before a witness who was no less a personage than Jupiter. Then a month's delay ensued, pending a satisfactory response. After that, if nothing was forthcoming from their opponent, the ambassadors would throw a javelin across the enemy's border, and war was declared. Later on, with Roman legions fighting on more and more distant battlegrounds, the authorities realised that it was becoming ridiculously expensive to keep sending these ambassadors from one end of the Empire to the other. So they hit on the brilliant idea of building a column just outside the Eternal City's boundaries, and telling the world that it represented the enemy's disputed border. This was a real breakthrough.

The Romans cannot claim exclusive rights to this legalistic approach to warfare. In ancient Mexico, three delegations had to be dispatched to your troublesome neighbours before you could begin fighting. If they failed, then you declared war with the utmost formality, including presents to the enemy. These people had style.

And the Incas had a propaganda machine which they employed before any declaration of war. They sent experts in technology and commerce to persuade rival nations that they would be better off accepting their rule and protection. According to historians, this method of gentle persuasion often gave the required result.

The Jews had a clear conception of what made a war legitimate. All wars waged on idolaters, enemies of the Hebrew religion, and anyone not lucky enough to belong to one of the twelve tribes united by a common faith and descendancy — all such wars were just. Add together all the people in those categories and you get quite a crowd.

Saint Augustine gave us the best insight into the Church's teaching: a war is quite acceptable to right a wrong, subdue a nation or increase your Empire. In the Middle Ages, writers improved on this by making the point that the justice of your action depends on the quality of leadership of the man declaring war. If he is the Holy Roman Emperor, the King of France or the Pope, it must be a just war. If on the other hand war is declared by a tinpot ruler, he is automatically in the wrong, even though he may have been the victim of all kinds of provocations.

Saint Thomas Aquinas followed in the footsteps of Saint Augustine: a war is justifiable if it is waged to regain what you have lost unjustly, or then again, if your enemy deserved to be attacked because of his actions. This opens up infinite possibilities.

Machiavelli and other thinkers of the sixteenth century went one stage further, with the statement that a just war is one which is necessary.

Later on, Francis de Victoria maintained that any state is entitled to wage war if its legitimate interests or national honour are in question. The question of patriotism has revealed the touchy nature of many countries. Furthermore, according to de Victoria, war in itself is not evil, as the terrible deeds done in its name occur by accident, and worse would follow if war was not allowed. He does not explain what.

As far as the Church is concerned, a just war is one waged on heretics and infidels. In this category is every fool, every luckless individual, every ignoramus or rebel who has not taken refuge in the one, true Church, universal, apostolic and Roman.

The finest legal minds of the end of the sixteenth century belonged to Pierre Belli, Alberic Gentili, Ayala and Guerreiro. The latter listed eleven circumstances where war is just, such as a war waged against pagan nations, or rebellious ones, or against people who insult king or ambassador, or to free oneself from an unfair treaty, or against a nation which is giving assistance to a potential rival, and so on. The list was extremely handy for princes with a shortage of troublesome neighbours.

Lastly the philosopher Grotius: war is justified if it is a question of protecting your property, of punishing offenders and of warding off a threat. One could say in a more general way that the ultimate justification, as far as Grotius is concerned, is the best interest of the state. This brings us back to Machiavelli and even to the ancient Greeks, who used to say that whatever was necessary to the nation was justifiable and all to the good. All history's military leaders invoked the interests of the state, from Louis XIV to Hitler, via Frederick the Great and Napoleon.

Although the world's finest legal and philosophical brains have given us these points of view, it has to be admitted that the sum total of their considerations appears to be something of a jumble, with some good reasons and above all a number of bad ones for the doctrine of a just war. Difficult as it is to come to a conclusion, we should try to approach the problem with as much simplicity as possible.

*   *   *

Anyone embarking on a war does so because he wants justice. It is therefore reasonable to suppose that deep down he believes his cause to be just. Naturally, he is keen to demonstrate this to the world, and so he will do all he can to give the impression of someone who is the innocent victim of a terrible aggressor. Few and far between are leaders who will go to war calling a spade a spade, ready to admit that what they want is a neighbour's riches, or new trading markets, natural resources or new lands to exploit. Clovis is said to have told his men: "Follow me, and I will take you to places where you will find gold and silver." Napoleon would harangue his troops: "Soldiers, you are badly fed and almost naked . . . I shall take you to the world's richest valleys, where you will find great cities and wealthy provinces; and there you will gain honour, glory and riches." On the eve of the First World War, the German Max Harden declared: "We need land for our farmers, free highways and openings to the sea." Thirty years later Goebbels was the one to say: "We are fighting this war for wheat and bread . . . for essential needs, for rubber, oil, iron and steel."

Such moments of candour are rare. Hitler himself, not so simple as his spokesman, did his best to cloak his military ambitions in a respectable mantle. He was only following in the footsteps of all leaders taking the offensive, whose task is to come up with an excuse which has all the hallmarks of sincerity, virtuous indignation and a sense of fair play under grievous attack.

This is not as difficult a task as one might think. Suitable avenues open up in three main directions:

1. The enemy's territories can be made to look badly developed and run down and their inhabitants appearing unworthy of such lands. This could be known as the 'casting pearl before swine' method. Judgement is swift: "When a nation is seen to be incapable of exploiting the land which nature has awarded it, it must give way to others."[3]
2. A gallant response to a cry for help from an oppressed minority, suffering under an unscrupulous foe. Such was Chancellor Hitler's reaction when he leapt to the assistance of the German minorities in Austria, Czechoslovakia and Poland, thus displaying brotherly love. He was unaware that he was using the same formula as Rome had done before him, when nations which she had apparently defended found themselves under the yoke.
3. But there is no doubt that of all possible reasons the best is legitimate self-defence. This can occur in a number of ways:

   a) The extreme case is when you are *forced to defend yourself against ignorance, stubbornness and ill will*. Here is a dialogue between a white man and a Red Indian, by the philosopher J. Novicow:

   The White Man — I would like to improve the yield of some
       fields which you are not exploiting sufficiently.
   The Indian — But I would no longer be able to hunt across
       them and I would starve.
   The White Man — No. I would teach you how to live very
       comfortably on a holding 7,600 times smaller than the one
       you need today.
   The Indian — No thanks. I do not want to change my
       lifestyle. I want to live as my ancestors did. I will not sell
       you my lands. Please leave.
   The White Man — Well, if one of us must starve to death, I
       would rather it was you. You did not accept a peaceful
       liberation, so prepare for a military one!

   Novicow goes on with the utmost seriousness: "It looks as if the White Man is the aggressor. But in truth the Indian is. The White Man offers him money, then the chance to improve his lot materially, in exchange for his land. The Indian should have welcomed the White Man with open arms. But the Indian is reluctant to adapt to a new social environment. He wants to keep things as they are, and is willing to let the White Man starve to death. Therefore he seeks to damage the White Man's condition, which makes any act of war against the Indian perfectly legitimate."

b) *You are the victim of an actual aggression*, but only after you have consistently provoked your opponent, with a series of outbursts against his national pride, of ridiculous demands, of gross insults, of lies, threats, and acts of hostility. Until at last, his patience exhausted, his self-respect in shreds, your opponent draws his sword, fearful for the safety of his country.

c) *You pretend you have come under attack.* One of the best examples of this is Napoleon I, who was foolhardy enough to trust historians when writing his memoirs. He believed they would accept his premise that far from liking war too much, he had "invariably" been "the victim of aggression".[4] Similarly, there is no question that if the Soviet Union had to steel herself to invade Finland in 1939, it was because her powerful neighbour had attacked her first, and gallant little Russia was defending herself justly.

d) *We were about to be attacked.* Preventive wars, which Frederick the Great called "wars of precaution", and which "princes sensibly must undertake. Better to anticipate before someone else anticipates first." Montesquieu claimed it was necessary to attack a neighbour if peace was lasting long enough for him to build up his destructive resources, and that such an attack would be the only way to prevent destruction.

Many leaders have obeyed these principles, and done well as a result. Others, less fortunate, were unable to put their ideas into practice; either because they did not inspire sufficient confidence, or because they came up against the people's fearfulness, or simply because they lacked authority. Such, for instance, is the case of the American, General Gow, who kept a personal diary. Here are some excerpts which relate to the "war of prevention" which he proposed to wage against the Soviet Union: "5 Feb. 1951: We must start by hitting below the belt. This war cannot be conducted according to Marquess of Queensberry rules. (27 March) War! As soon as possible! Now! (29 March) It seems to me the time is ripe for a blow this year."

The same hope was expressed by Dr. Robert Montgomery, professor at Texas University. "I am not worried about the Russians. I am worried about us. If we have to kill them, we should do it now, and not wait three years . . . In twenty-four hours we could wipe 75 million Russians off the face of the earth for the loss of only 100 of our own men."

That is how golden opportunities slip through our fingers, never to return.

It should be noted that a preventive war, which involves taking action against a potential enemy before he has done anything to offend us, and in which we claim his intentions were bad, is actually an act of self-defence. This argument can be taken a little further by claiming that all wars must appear to be waged in self-defence, whatever their origins and purposes, whatever their ultimate aim. All of which explains why most governments today have no War Ministry as they used to, but do have a Ministry of Defence instead.

It is as though politicians and military leaders were somehow ashamed of revealing their true selves — ambitious, warlike, seeking after glory and triumphs. They know — who better? — that it would be ridiculous to let your enemy invade and lay waste your nation's land, that on the contrary you must take the battle to him if you want to crush him, and as has been said so often, the best form of defence is attack.

But what about international public opinion, which has to be respected? The expansion of all types of media has made it much more important. It has replaced the old religion-based moral values, and it represents the layman's code of honour, his well-ordered diplomacy, and political loyalty. Any country which manages to get public opinion on its side can expect money, weapons, and allies to back it at the UN or on the battlefield. The Press, the Church and honest men will lend their support. Its fighting men will enjoy the best possible morale, certain of world-wide approval. Its leaders will themselves get taken in eventually, and end up with clear consciences.

It is essential for a state engaging in warfare to appear to everyone as the victim of another's aggression. They must accumulate as many examples of it as possible in all patience, must find bona fide witnesses, preferably from one or other superpower, and must act quickly to stem any rumours which might cause them embarrassment. Naturally, the enemy will do the same. They too will try to show they are innocent of any aggression, that theirs was never a warlike intent, that they were taken by surprise, and their good faith cannot be put into question.

At this juncture, things become complicated. For if one party can claim legitimate self-defence, then the other must have carried out an attack. Yet, on this point, both parties are quite positive: neither attacked.

To try to throw some light on this confusion, let us take an example. On 5th June 1967, at 7.24, a telegram from Tel Aviv states: "This morning, Egypt attacked Israel in the south with tanks and planes."

The same day, at the same time, Cairo radio says: "Israeli troops launched an attack on us this morning."

Six years later, on 9th October 1973, Israeli radio declares: "Today at one o'clock, enemy forces launched an attack in the Sinai and on the Golan heights."

On their side, Cairo radio says: "Israeli enemy troops attacked our men at 12.30. We are fighting back against the invading forces."

And Damascus radio broadcasts: "At one o'clock, Israeli troops attacked our positions all the way along the ceasefire line."

In other words, the protagonists of both the six-day war and the war of Yom Kippur accused each other of starting the fighting.

Eventually, both sides admitted that Israel began it in 1967 and the Arab countries did so in 1973. Should we naively assume that the Jews lied in 1967 and the Egyptians and Syrians lied in 1973? The problem is more complex than that. Referring back to what we said earlier about a preventive war, it seems that the six day war in 1967 fits the case perfectly. Leaving aside the blockade of the Gulf of Aquaba, a typically hostile act according to international law, Israel was threatened on every frontier by a three-state coalition, which for several weeks had been harassing her with warlike slogans and threats to wipe out the Jewish state.

In other words, if the aggressor is the one who first takes up arms and invades enemy territory, then Israel is at fault. If, on the other hand, the fault lies with those who bring the attack on themselves because of provocation and threats, then the alliance of Arab states should be considered the true aggressor.

Turning to the Yom Kippur war, we find a military operation

aimed at recouping territory annexed by the enemy, which he
stubbornly refused to give up despite a number of diplomatic
moves and strongly worded international resolutions. Looked
at that way, the Arab states were perfectly in their right to take up
arms. But if you place the blame firmly on the shoulders of the
ones who fired first, there is no doubt that the Arabs were the
aggressors.

The split in international opinion at the time shows how
difficult it is to apportion responsibility between the protagonists.

Russia believed the events were "a direct result of continued
Israeli aggression". Britain declared "the Arab states are
responsible for the aggression." Yugoslavia "condemns Israeli
aggression". France's M. Defferre thought "the Egyptians and
Syrians are responsible for the war. They attacked first." In
India, Mrs. Indira Gandhi put "entire blame for the fighting on
Israel." The correspondent of "National Zeitung" in Basle
wrote: "Do not look in Tel Aviv or Washington for those
responsible for sparking off the conflict . . . Look in Cairo."

Are these conflicting views so surprising? It would seem not if
one accepts that there is equal confusion about responsibility
for starting a war in most cases. This applies to Korea, Pakistan
and Cambodia, a country invaded by Vietnamese forces bent
on self-defence and "the punishment of aggressors", according
to Hanoi's ambassador. After all, discussion still goes on over
who was responsible for starting the First World War, and that
despite a large number of theses, tomes and articles published
over the last sixty years which have failed to clear the matter
up.

It has to be said that defining aggression is no easy matter.
There are numerous different opinions. With their firm and
ancient belief in custom and practice, Anglo-Saxons prefer to
examine each case on its own merit, suspicious of any general
formula, and this hallowed system has had plenty of success,
well recognised. Other nations, including France, prefer
beautifully articulated abstract declarations, which have the
drawback of equally theoretical terms which form the basis of
endless polemical debates.

Yet others, such as the Soviet Union, like to list all provocative
acts, but however long the list they will always have one
unexpected case missing. It has been noted too that beyond the
relatively obvious case of armed attack exist such acts as
blockading ports, assaults by sea, overflying enemy territory,

waging a war of propaganda including making use of racialist insults, supporting subversion, intimidation, imposing commercial tariff barriers, and so on. No surprise then that eminent lawyers of the League of Nations who ventured into this vipers' nest from 1923 to 1936, and that equally eminent lawyers working for the United Nations from 1950 to 1957, attempting to sort things out anew, came to the conclusion after twenty years of special commissions, sub-commissions, committees and sub-committees, that they could sort nothing out at all.

Is this reason enough to give up, as some do, any hope of being able to put forward a clear definition? We believe not. On the contrary, we believe that by shedding light as we have done with the above argument, in all modesty we have found a definition which sidesteps all the difficulties and answers every criticism. Simple enough to be universally understood, it has the merit of being brief, is general and yet specific, all-inclusive, and by taking in every possible permutation, makes any distinctions superfluous. We would like to propose this definition to international legislators so that it can be absorbed into current diplomatic thinking, and it is this: the aggressor is always somebody else. This enables both protagonists inevitably to be acting in self-defence, and their good faith cannot be questioned. This leads us to the logical consequence that war is always just on both sides.

This was the conclusion reached by Joseph Proudhon when he wrote: "the nature of war, national motives, declared ambitions, and the overtly legalistic form in which it is conducted, indicate that it is not only no more unjust on one side than the other, but jointly and separately equally just."

Before him, the philosopher Alciat, Molina the Hermit and many others had backed this point of view. In our day the Church defends a similar position even though it is not in the habit of challenging world public opinion by taking up a revolutionary position, tending rather to sin through excessive caution.

To illustrate this sentiment, we have accumulated statements made by a large number of heads of state and military leaders of all kinds. These have been edited into a coherent speech — if you like, the prototype of all calls to arms. The fact that you cannot pick out disagreements from within shows that the enemy camps recognise implicitly that war is justified on both sides at once, and so use the same arguments.

Suggested speech to be used on Declaration of War.
(Being a compilation of extracts from speeches by World Leaders.)

The hour of battle has struck (Sadat). We send fraternal greetings to our forces on the seas, in the air and on land, all of whom, standing by at their battle posts, are ready to enter the fray (Churchill). May all be ready to make the sacrifice required, may you all serve your country to the best of your ability (Hitler). Everyone will have his chance for glory, even the most feeble (Clemenceau). Our civilians will also play their part to the full. They are motivated by strong wills, discipline and hope (Lebrun). Heads held high and with a clear conscience, our people march into danger. Faithful to our motto, who dares wins (Herriot).

How comforting it is to be able to recall today all the efforts we made to keep the peace (Churchill). This is a war we never wanted (Hitler). We said and did everything possible to avoid it (Clemenceau). It was forced upon us (Daladier). There can be no doubt as to which side has justice (Wilhelm II). We have taken up arms that justice may triumph (Goebbels). If we fight today, it is for our people's very existence (Daladier). Our troops are there to protect all that we have. They are fighting to defend the nation, its artistic and cultural independence (Goebbels). To protect our territorial integrity and national honour (Mrs. Gandhi). Yes, we are fighting for our nation's integrity and its honour (General Khan, Pakistan).

Never have their been such clear reasons for going to war than in present circumstances . . . We fight not just (Reynaud) for the safety, liberty and independence of our nation (Stalin) but for all mankind, not just this generation, but all generations to come (F.D. Roosevelt). We believe with all our hearts in the cause of justice, of prosperity, of progress and peace for the entire human race (Hitler).

It is our good fortune to fight to establish peace in the world (Woodrow Wilson). A just and lasting peace (Eden). This is our real goal: to work towards a world more just and at peace (Truman), towards a lasting future peace (Wilhelm II).

We remain steadfast and resolved (Daladier). We have no doubt at all about the victory to come (Mrs Meir). It will be our reward for moral strength and perseverance. The complete defeat of the enemy (Poincaré), that is the goal towards which all our efforts must be directed (Daladier). Our duty is war; victory is to come (de Gaulle).

We put our trust in the Almighty (Wilhelm II). God is with us (Greek government 1974), with our rightful cause (Wilhelm I). May He bless our troops! (Turkish government 1974). May He protect us and bring our warlike efforts to a successful outcome (Chatel, governor-general of Algeria). May He make our people and our soldiers strong enough to achieve their tasks with fortitude and bravery, that we may be saved (Hitler). We must be united, we must be undaunted, we must be determined (Churchill). We can win, we must win, we will win (Goebbels).

Chapter 3
Short and Sweet

Human beings have never been strong on logic. In every generation, there have always been people ready to condemn out of hand the cruel suffering war brings, while they accept that men must kill each other in a normal world. Fair enough, make the omelette, they say, but do not break the eggs.

Let us try to make sense of this. We have seen that the protagonists, certain their cause is the right one, can have only one objective — victory, at any price. To quote Clausewitz: "Philanthropic-minded souls may fondly imagine there is some artificial way to defeat and disarm your enemy with little bloodshed . . . This is a mistake which must be put right . . . It is impossible and absurd to hope to introduce a moderating influence in war. War is an act of violence, and there are no limits to this violence." That much is clear. It would be as ridiculous to ask a soldier to conquer with caution, to exterminate politely, to pillage with good breeding, as it would be to set limits to a fire once lit. One would have to be extraordinarily naive, or totally lacking in good faith, to maintain the opposite.

In any event, history tells the truth. In the two World Wars, every single solemn undertaking was violated by the great powers. Commercial shipping was torpedoed, gas was used, cities were bombed, hostages executed, civilians massacred.

In any future war, no agreement will be respected, however many long and difficult months of negotiation precede its ratification, whether it bans a particular weapon or a method of extermination. It only needs one protagonist to discover it is to his advantage to break the agreement.

You only need to show that methods employed, however base, are a necessary part of your overall strategy, and the thing is done. Nothing could be easier and less taxing mentally. Take the example of the German chief of staff: "Any action, no matter how barbarous, can be justified by military exigencies" (German High Command 1914). And there it is.

With our moral standing safe, we can choose the most effective weapons, which means the most lethal, since "anything goes", and "the battle must be bloody, and every blow decisive", and warfare itself "legalises and sanctifies every method of waging it".[5]

More often than not, the combatants have no choice, and from one move to the next they are pushed inexorably into worse extremes of behaviour. One curious thing is that there are always valid reasons why such escalation should occur. Any commander-in-chief who witnesses appalling setbacks and sees his reserves melting away before his eyes, and who knows that defeat is staring him in the face, will play his ace card. He has nothing more to lose, and if he can produce from his chemical laboratories some dreadful new agent of death, he will. On the other hand, if he sees victory within his grasp, if the enemy's men are running away or on the point of mutiny, if their downfall is only a question of time, why should he hesitate to help things along a little with some unmentionable weapon of destruction? Wisely he may consider that victory will legitimise his action. Marshal Keitel used to tell his men: "It is not only justifiable but our duty as soldiers to use all methods open to us without exception, even against women and children, as long as we gain victory as a result." In this context, we may now examine the usefulness of pillaging, laying waste, individual cruelty such as rape and torture, execution of prisoners, of wounded men and hostages, and lastly the massacre of civilians.

Pillage

Cicero wrote: "It is human nature to loot a man's body when you have killed him justly." Before him, Greek philosophers were of the same opinion. Aristotle classifies pillage as a light industry, in the same category as agriculture. The Romans gave more consideration to a pirate than to a shopkeeper. Lawyers of the middle ages as well as of 17th and 18th centuries also accepted the right to booty, and maintained that God himself had given His whole-hearted approval to this practice. Pillage could even be considered as the origin of ownership. This is obvious because most languages have only one word to express both plunder and possession. In Hebrew, the same word expresses the concepts of the hunt and of gain. In Tahitian, the word 'taho' means both spear and property, which must lead to a number of misunderstandings. In Sanskrit, hearing the word 'Ga-vishtu', you would not be clear whether to go to war or out looking for your cows.

Pillage is a soldier's reward. If a siege had proved particularly long and difficult, troops were promised one or more days of pillage.It often happened that soldiers were paid in booty only, in the way that certain employees today are paid only in tips. An argument was put forward that mercenaries found it less insulting to receive booty rather than a wage, and they much preferred the former, it being easier for their sensitive natures to accept and no doubt also likely to yield greater rewards.

These days, soldiers are paid a salary, but one has to admit that their wages are modest considering they have to risk their lives for the rest of us. It would seem reasonable, then, that they should be entitled to a further reward, as long as they are not killed before they can collect.

Two types of pillaging exist. The first is the individual, chaotic kind, born out of the fury of battle or its conclusion, with or without the blessing of the leadership. Its characteristics are a certain virility combined with a childlike innocence, a bit roustabout, quite likeable, really. The idea is to grab without calculating their worth any objects, provisions or drink that come to hand. Certain ravages that may occur are understood in the context of the atmosphere in which the pillaging takes place. After all, the men committing the pillage could at any moment fall victim to a sniper's bullet. Or they could simply be taken by surprise by the houseowner who might have some odd idea of defending his property. Speed is essential.

An ordinary burgler's precautions are not suitable. There is no point in looking for keys to cupboards, or the number of a safe. Best to smash them open with a rifle butt, a bayonet or, if necessary, blow them open with a grenade. The furniture may suffer a little, but such is war, and really it is of no importance since before they leave, they will set the house on fire.

History is rife with tales of plunder. The Romans pillaged conquered nations, Crusaders pillaged the Infidels, during the Hundred Years' War 'scorchers' ripped clothes from their victims' bodies, and one of the most famous acts of pillage was the sacking of the Summer Palace in Pekin by Anglo-French troops in 1860. "Artillerymen stuffed their cannon-mouths full of gold pieces. Footsoldiers filled their powder pouches with them . . . You cannot imagine to what furious lengths they pushed their mania for pillage."[6] Much the same can be said of

our 'acts of war' in the colonies, whether it be the Indian sub-
continent for Britain, or north Africa for France. It was expected
of our troops, according to the fashion of the day.

The French Revolution and Bonaparte developed a more
elaborate form of pillage, better known as requisition and the
cost of occupation. Unbelievable as it may seem, it was quite
common to see soldiers starving to death yards from farms full
of provisions. That was before the Revolution. All such taboos
were swept away by the French republican generals and after
them, the Imperial troops. War must feed war, declared
Napoleon, who was always at the forefront of progress. Very
soon the art of pillaging went beyond the acquisition of
provisions into the industrial and cultural domains. Here too
Bonaparte led the field. He wrote: "the Arts Commission has
achieved a good haul in Ravenna, Rimini and Pesaro, all of
which will be sent on to you. Add to that what you will be
receiving from Rome, and we will possess all that is finest in
Italy." A century and a half later, some of these masterpieces
were to travel in a new direction, this time from France to
Germany, under the auspices of Marshal Goering.

Today's state-to-state collective form of pillage has not
replaced individual looting. They co-exist, though the latter is
tolerated only, while the former has acquired an official look
about it through its need for sophisticated systems of operation.
Among other measures are a special coinage, fixed and arbitrary
exchange rates, enforced exports, state control of distribution
outlets and so on.

Between 1940 and 1944, the Germans 'bought' agricultural
produce and clothing in France worth a total of 350 billion
francs, following this principle, plus another billion marks in
return for the cost of occupying the country. They presented
Denmark and Norway with bills of indemnity totalling some 11
billion crowns.

Out in the open or under the counter, individual or
collective, the act of pillaging is above all a military necessity. It
has several uses. As we have seen, the first function is to ensure
the all-important transfer of property which gives the winning
side substantial booty and allows them to grow in confidence,
while the enemy are thrown into confusion at the same time,
and their territory's roads become choked with ruined
refugees, homeless, starving and terrified creatures. Secondly, if
the enemy's lands can be occupied and looting organised on an

altogether grander scale, there can be no doubt that the short-term effect on the nation's health with severe rationing in force, and the long-term effect on the country's general economy can only be beneficial to the cause by hastening victory. Finally, freedom to loot is an important factor in a soldier's psychological stability, and hence in an army's morale. After days and nights of anguish, of nervous tension and exhaustion, he will achieve peace in his soul more easily with such freedom than by practising sport or yoga. Judging it to be a way of indulging in destructive instincts or dubious desires would be quite false. On the contrary, it is a perfectly healthy and normal activity which exists under the surface in all of us.

Destruction

The First World War had already accounted for the destruction of a number of homes and historic buildings, and such towns as Arras, Soissons and Rheims bore witness to the conflict. Entire villages laid waste, roads torn up, bridges destroyed, forests cut down, reservoirs blown up, castles still standing after centuries turned into historic ruins. But there are geographical limits to the ravaged areas, and this is still on an amateur level.

A new ball-game emerges with the Second World War, and after it the war in Vietnam. The nerve centres are Rotterdam, London, Coventry, Hamburg, Dresden, Berlin, Tokyo, Hanoi. This time, whole cities are pulverised, residential areas as well as industrial. The closer we get to perfect war, or what Ludendorff called total war, the more blurred become differences between civilians and soldiers. The entire population is responsible.

That goes for a simple piano teacher in Cologne, blown up in the middle of a lesson along with his pupil, his wife and two children. It goes for a bank clerk in the City, who goes up in smoke along with his elderly mother. It goes for the seven twisted corpses of the Nguyen van Si family in Hanoi — husband, wife, two little daughters, an adolescent youth, and the little boy, still clutching a baby to his body. Good health, ladies and gentlemen. There are no more exceptions, no excuses, no alibis. No-one is exempt. Hospitals can be bombed since they cure fighting men wounded in battle. Maternity hospitals can be bombed too, since they breed new enemies. Schools can be bombed, since they educate today's youth to become tomorrow's troops. Churches can be bombed, since the faithful can find comfort there to prolong the battle.

Undermining the foundations of a museum or library is a way of undermining your enemy's morale, by cutting him off from his cultural past. That is the very point of such destruction — to break down the people's resistance, wear them down, reduce their productivity, cause chaos in their public services. In a word, terrorise them.

Rape

Rape is the logical next step after pillage. Since time immemorial, men have possessed women just as they possess their furniture, and as such, women have been classed as objects of pleasure or useful workers for carrying out household chores. To the conqueror, his enemy's goods, to do with as he pleases. The only reproach one can make to the soldier who rapes his victims is that he is offending against Christian morals and committing a sin. But that is what confession is for. Rape is and always has been acceptable, one of the inalienable rights of fighting men. A young subaltern on duty in Algeria told his squad: "Rape is allowed, but do it discreetly!" Unfortunately, his advice is not always followed. Soldiers do tend to be rather generous with their feelings. They like to share the fun — in one case a young Muslim girl was assaulted by twenty-five men. They like to give themselves with enthusiasm, whatever age their partner, be it a woman of a hundred or a child of eight. And it must be done with style, with a full house to admire their skill and prowess. They need the plaudits of the public. They are men of the theatre. They will invite the girl's family to the show, her husband, father, brothers, children young and old, cousins, friends. Their role is to give encouragement, support him in the difficult moments, applaud the final outcome. As for the partner herself, she will be expected to give a few encores with mercenaries and other ancillary troops, as long as she is not too tired after the principal performance.

Real poetry and romance of this kind is to be found among the French of course. The American GI has a less stylish approach. His is a practical one, and his philosophy can be (and was) summed up: "Our guys are real men."[7] A good example of this is the following story, which took place on 17 November 1966.

"A twenty-year-old sergeant, a veteran of three years in Vietnam, was on dawn patrol with his squad. They came to the village of Cat Huong in Phu My district. He told his men to search all the huts to find a woman they might take on their march to relieve the tension. In one hut they found a terrified mother with her two daughters. They liked the look of the older girl, Phim Ti Mao. Tying her hands behind her back, they dragged her off. Running behind them, the mother wept and begged them to stop. Seeing she could do nothing, she took off her shawl and held it out to the soldiers to put it on the shivering young girl. Amused, the sergeant snatched it from her and used it to gag the girl. One of the men strapped his kitbag to Phim Ti Mao's back and she followed the squad as best she could. Towards ten-thirty, they reached hill 192 where they came across an abandoned hovel. The five men stopped there and had something to eat, ignoring the girl, cowering and weeping in a corner. After his meal, the sergeant ripped off her clothes, tied her to a table abandoned there by the hut's last inhabitants, and raped her. Afterwards he let the others have their turn, and one of them idly scored her body with his knife."[8]

In this particular case, the girl was executed next day on the sergeant's orders, as she had seen too much for safety. But there are no fixed rules to this game.

Torture

Torture is essentially one means of discovering vital military information, but its use is limited. Victims have a deplorable habit of saying whatever comes into their heads so as to put an end to their suffering. This makes their statements virtually useless. Such a drawback should have made the practice of torture redundant long ago. Curiously, it has had the opposite effect. The reason is simple enough. The development of long-range artillery, fighter-bombers and tanks has removed combatants from any close contact. All they see now is a blip on a radar screen. But man needs that face-to-face confrontation, and the art of torture gives him his chance. It recreates the emotional, human touch lost in modern warfare. It puts an end to the desperation of anonymity. It establishes a truly intimate relationship between the victim and his tormentor.

It has been said rather flippantly that torture has a touch of sadism about it, allowing unacceptable passions to come to the fore. NCOs who torture prisoners (normally only NCOs and above are privileged enough to do so) are sometimes accused of pandering to their own prejudices against certain racial, professional or political categories. Instinctively, they feel this is their way to take revenge on people who might prove superior in intellectual ability. They concentrate their efforts on determined or brilliant victims, and the maddened will to kill which possesses them is the same as the impulse which swept through a crowd at the sight of an Early Martyr. At the same time inflicting such punishment on their victims makes them justify their jobs and their rank.

Not for us, the task of passing judgement about these allegations. No doubt it must have happened that third degree questioning has turned into personal revenge or sadism. This is often a natural development rather than a deliberate intent to do evil. The salient aspect of torture, as far as we can see, is its gamesmanship. It is an exercise in imagination, with no cheating, where the winner is chosen in advance. It has lost any strategic significance, acquiring instead supreme psychological importance. At this point, it becomes self-fulfilling, 'art for art's sake'.

Man's inventive spirit has played a primary role in the development of this art form. One can only admire his remarkable creativity, the wonderful sense of humour he has displayed. All this is evident from a glance at the various handbooks, pamphlets and articles which deal with torture. They are a joy to read. Naturally enough, in the first instance you come across the great classics — the wheel, on which you tied your victim after his bones had been broken; wooden boots which crushed his legs and feet to a pulp; a simple remedy for preventing him from crying out or talking too much — ripping out his tongue; cutting off penis or testicles — popular in the east but never a great favourite in the western world among God-fearing Christians who preferred red-hot irons, gibbets, the rack, and other methods which have survived until today, such as pulling off nails, caging your victims, pouring vinegar into their nostrils, or more simply the well-loved water treatment, still much in use.

These are the classic methods, and side by side with them, man's fertile imagination has invented a whole range of sophisticated forms of torture, some of which are absolutely hilarious. Here are a number of examples.

The Turks came up with an ingenious way of extracting a confession. The victim was first made to eat a large quantity of delicious water melon. That was no problem. Gradually though, he would discover the fruit's qualities, and he would gladly have let nature take her course if his captors had not tied him up so comprehensively that there was no question of passing water.

In England, where good sense and caution prevail, torture victims would have a red-hot poker thrust into their bowels, but it would first go through a tube made of horn so as not to leave any burn marks on the skin.

Then there was Suleiman the Magnificent, who invented a new kind of court entertainment. The victim was tied to a plank and small holes were made all over his body with a sharp dagger. Into these oil was poured, a wick was placed, and lo and behold, a very original kind of birthday cake! It is said that the emperor, presented with these unusual gifts, greeted them with enthusiastic applause.

Torture almost disappeared in Europe in the nineteenth century, but made its comeback in the twentieth. Relying on tradition, nevertheless it did not hesitate to make use of modern science, in particular electricity, developments in medical knowledge and especially drugs. Usage extended to the science of acquiring information even in peace-time, but that is outside our parameters.

The finest hour of torture came with the Gestapo during the Second World War. It was given official sanction by Himmler in an edict dated 12 June 1942, authorising the use of third degree to force confessions and essential information from prisoners. Men were trained for this specialist work through intensive month-long courses which included medical, practical and academic subjects. Qualified Nazi technicians then proceeded to add technological developments to well-tried methods. Theirs is the credit for first providing medical supervision to ensure victims did not die prematurely in the course of an interrogation.

This sensible precaution reduced the accident rate substantially. Between 1940 and 1945, the number of people who died during questioning in French prisons was only just over forty thousand.

Torture as defined by the Nazi leadership has grown in popularity, acquiring on the way national 'folksy' characteristics. The Japanese used their enemies as dummies for bayonet practice. The Vietnamese, later on, harnessed French prisoners by means of rings through their noses and led them, two by two, through their villages. At each stopping-place, a wooden splinter was thrust into each man's cheek, and when eventually their heads looked like pincushions, they were cut off.

The West is not far behind. French and then Americans, when they were not bombing with napalm, were torturing their enemies, and to ensure the loyalty of the South Vietnamese they forced them to execute the Viet-Cong publicly. One French general wrote to another: "Vietnam is our great opportunity. This will be a historic moment for our nation".

Beware though of a certain romanticism about torture, as well as of a tendency to exaggeration by sensitive natures. To take a recent example, the Algerian war was neither better nor worse than any other conflict. One French general put it into perspective: "I believe that generally our men behaved like choirboys, and a good thing too. If on occasions they had to 'have a go' to make someone cough up, they only used the amount of force necessary with occasionally just a touch of violence, all that was necessary to acquire immediate information without in any way debasing the individual."[9]

Nothing debasing indeed about the sack — a method by which the victim is lifted up with a rope and pulley and dropped brutally; or the game of football, in which the ball is the victim, blindfolded, and the players are soldiers wearing hob-nailed boots.

Torture is a widespread phenomenon in this age. Since the Second World War it has been used as much by highly industrialised nations as by developing countries. British forces in Ireland used the five-point method (prisoners hooded and subjected to loud noises, made to stand long hours without food or sleep), Israeli experts are believed to have invented a chemical which produces severe mental disorders, and every single NATO army, leaving aside the world's other forces, has specialised units trained to extract information through 'in-depth' interrogation.

Executions and Massacres

Killing off prisoners-of-war is not always the answer; sometimes it is better to make slaves out of them. The writer Grotius explains that in order to persuade a victorious army to spare the lives of prisoners, rather than killing them, to which extreme act they were entitled by their victory, certain institutions had been created. For instance, the law by which a master was owner, not just of a slave and his goods, but of all his descendants for evermore. It follows that from a business point of view, it makes more sense to employ such people as labourers, farm hands, navvies and miners, than to execute them. German military leaders during the last world war understood this, and set up systems of forced labour for civilians, prisoners-of-war and deportees. Such a work force, virtually limitless in numbers, easily pleased and cost-effective, represented a substantial asset for the Third Reich. Salt mines, steel works and factories turning out ovens, bricks and such like material were particular beneficiaries.

It remained the case that any workers proving difficult to supervise, or found to be lazy, or low in productivity, or dangerous to the security of the state and the welfare of those around them, could simply be put to death. Everyone agrees on this point, and it has always been accepted — among primitive tribes and the nations of Antiquity alike — that prisoners who prove to be a nuisance should be killed off. The same thing was said in an official document by the German High Command in 1902. "Prisoners may be killed . . . in absolutely necessary cases when no means of guarding them is available and their presence constitutes a real danger to their captors."

History is peppered with instances of hostages being executed. This is a good place to quote from a letter written by that great French genius, Napoleon Bonaparte, to his brother Joseph, whom he had made a king, and who had to cope with insurrection: "Security in your kingdom will depend on how you assert yourself in the conquered territories. Put to the torch a dozen villages which are holding out against you, once they have been properly looted, of course. My soldiers must not return empty-handed! Hang three or even six people from each village involved, and do not spare the clergy. Remember what I achieved in Corsica."

With such an illustrious example to follow, others have not hesitated. Nevertheless, after a timid start in 1914–18, it was not until the Second World War that the art of taking hostages flowered as an essential part of modern-day strategic warfare. It goes without saying that the effect of doing away with certain elements is in inverse proportion to the importance of their role in the continuing battle. Executing a prisoner-of-war, who is necessarily a combatant, and whose primary function is to die sooner or later, is obviously less spectacular than killing a hostage, who is an unarmed civilian. But executing people of no note, people without any particular identity, of both sexes and all ages, that surely is the finest achievement of military prowess.

The history of man is rife with massacres. The Hebrews killed the wives and children of the tribes of Hebron and Canaan. The Roman general Scipio ordered the massacre of every man, woman and child of Numantis. In the Punic Wars, the Roman army encircled the camp of Asdrubal and murdered all the Carthaginians there as well as their auxiliary troops, who were Gauls. They were asleep, drunk, on their straw mattresses. Even in those days, drink was a killer.

In the 12th century — the age of elegance — Barbarossa roamed Italy at the head of his army, cutting off 200 noses here, 200 lips there, two dozen right hands elsewhere, gouging out an eye here, hanging a victim there. For their part, the Italians had the curious habit of eating their enemies' hearts, and opening up their stomachs and using them as nosebags for their horses. It is said that even the equable Swiss, believe it or not, indulged in some carnage, and the future founders of the International Red Cross made a point of killing the sick in their hospital beds. In Cuba, army officers went to the theatre to shoot members of the audience, thus creating a more interesting spectacle off the stage than on it.

In the last century, western powers were operating in China (Britain, France, Germany and Russia) and the Emperor Wilhelm II instructed his troops: "No mercy. No prisoners. Just as the Huns under the leadership of Attila made a name for themselves a thousand years ago, so now the German name must last in China for another thousand years, to such an extent that no Chinaman will ever dare to look askance at a German." His instructions were followed. German soldiers wrote to their parents: "We went into their houses and finished them off with bayonets and rifle butts. They didn't even fight, they knelt down, kissed the ground and begged for mercy, but it was a waste of time. The captain had told us — no mercy. Women, men, children, all of them cut down with our sabres . . . When we manage to find a Chinaman on his own, we make him strip and then beat him to death with bamboo sticks." The Russians, for their part, played one or two games, such as throwing babies in the air and catching them on their bayonets, like kebabs on a skewer.

The same kind of burlesques were performed in more contemporary wars, such as Algeria and Vietnam. Such and such a colonial family massacred in Algeria. Bells tolling for villages razed by French fighter planes, or elsewhere, men bleeding to death in knife attacks, children crushed by tanks, women doused in petrol and burnt alive. A passing comment remembered: a young soldier says to his comrades after shooting a Muslim prisoner in the back — "he was lucky, I made him turn his head towards Mecca when I shot him." A sargeant comments, on slitting the throat of a victim — "I feel better. I had a real itch to make him smile from ear to ear!"

Though these quips may be a little tasteless, they are surely not worth the publicity they are given, any more than Vietnam's My Lai massacre deserves such notoriety (see Appendix II). Dozens of similar trifles happen in war without further ado. The man in the street knows full well how to put such things into perspective, and two years after Vietnam, 65% of Americans were to say that these incidents are inevitable in wartime. Who is going to get worked up about a few young lads having some target practice, and just four or five hundred dead — many of them in any case elderly and useless, many women and children?

It has to be admitted, however, that during the Second World War the Nazis were in a different league. Even as they exploited the gift of slave labour that fell into their hands, they organised an extraordinary operation for a particular category of individuals. This operation was conceived and carried out in the utmost calm, with far-sighted aims and objectives. In that, it contrasted with old-fashioned, fevered butcheries, haphazard, mindless, in the heat of the moment, amidst the ravages of Genghis Khan or Tamberlaine, in the frenzied massacre of more than a million souls at the fall of Jerusalem, or the furious slaughter of Armenians by the Turks. The extent of this operation, its grandiose concept of the elimination of an entire people, the scale of the undertaking as well as its scientific methods employed, all of this indicates a project which could be named Wagnerian in its scope. It could have been called the twilight of the Jews — it very nearly turned into their Endless Night.

Nor were the Hebrew people the only victims — Soviets, Czechs, Poles, Yugoslavs, Gypsies, all suffered the same fate. But the Jews had to pay the highest price, for two reasons. First, because in the words of Chancellor Hitler, Jews are "an inferior race which breeds like vermin, without the abilities of creative races . . . made up of monsters, missing links between men and apes." Monsters such as Jesus Christ, Spinoza, Heine, Chagall, Mendelssohn, Chaplin and Einstein.

Secondly, and apparently in contradiction to the above, this decadent, debased, servile race, which could be thought to be inoffensive, represents a terrible threat. Goebbels said "the total extermination of Europe's Jews is not a moral problem, but a question of the security of the state. Jews intend to take political and economic power, reducing non-Jewish peoples to slavery, and eventually doing away with them. They stop at nothing, and such is their wickedness that no-one should be surprised to see a Jew as the personification of the Devil among our people, representing everything that is evil." In other words, a Jew equals Satan.

From that time on, in Germany and occupied countries, it is open season for hunting the Devil. Raids, arrests, detention centres, followed by cattle trucks carrying one hundred and twenty victims each, to take them to the death camp. Inside these trucks, not much air, no food, no water. On arrival the tally is reasonable, only twenty-five percent dead.

Great names are on everyone's lips — Dachau, Ravensbruck, Auschwitz, Buchenwald. These are the meeting-points for the sub-human races. Death factories work overtime, machines running smoothly, gas rushing into locked chambers, ovens roaring, chimneys black with smoke.

Life goes on outside, and those charged with responsibility for the 'final solution' meet, have lunch, talk about their families, ask after each other's little ones. Men like Himmler, Mengele, Eichmann. After the pudding, some brandy and the talk turns to business. A new gas chamber has just been installed at Auschwitz, capable of accommodating two thousand people. This could be helpful to prevent a blockage in the detention centres. Will there be enough Zyklon B for full capacity? The discussion moves on to the special death lorries. These are now being recognised by victims in the queue, which creates panic. Why not disguise them to look like gypsy caravans with false porthole windows? Someone reads out a memo from Berlin: "operators are trying to force the pace by opening up the gas to its full extent. This means the victims die of suffocation instead of becoming unconscious. In fact, if the gas is kept half shut, they will die faster and more calmly. Open bowels and convulsed faces will no longer be seen." There is a silence.

The man in charge speaks up: "That's fine, then. Please ensure that all such instructions are properly followed. We must obey the regulations." The meal is coming to an end. Cigars all round, and then goodbyes with plenty of Heil Hitlers. There is work to be done.

The 'grand design' is taking shape. Eleven million human beings are scheduled for extermination in the plan. There must be no waste, says the Nazi directive. The maximum should be recuperated — glasses, gold and false teeth (no small economies) — and what is left of their bones can be used to manufacture fertiliser; fat is good for making soap, hair will do admirably to make slippers for submariners or thick soles of shoes for railworkers. You have to admire the attention to detail demonstrated. One memorandum on 6th August 1942 stipulates that men's hair must be at least twenty millimetres long to be of use. It concludes by saying: "Reports on the amount of hair collected from men and women must be filed on the 5th of each month, beginning 5th September 1942."

The camp residents made themselves useful in another way — by taking part in fascinating medical experiments. Frightened little shopkeepers discovered the thrill of high altitude flying as they were placed in an increasing vacuum until their lungs burst. Others were queuing up to sample phosgene and other gases, to be burnt with phosphorus, or injected with yellow fever, cholera or gangrene. Some volunteers were made to inject themselves with enough phenol to strike them down in seconds, so as to simulate euthanasia, in an experiment designed to help dying Germans meet their Maker with a smile on their lips. One or two refugees were singled out for the supreme honour of trying out the suicide capsules reserved for the High Command.

The Nazi medical authorities also tested a number of systems designed to prevent any chaotic proliferation of second-class races — Jews, Negroes, Slavs, Gypsies. These included a chemical injection to promote impotence in men, and simple castration, whether by surgery, injection, or X-rays. This last promised well, and Himmler in person was full of enthusiasm: "The mere thought that three million Bolshevik prisoners might be sterilised and yet remain active for forced labour, with no chance of propagating themselves, opens up enormous potential."

Women were not exempt from research. Many disabled Germans were given back the use of their legs thanks to the brave women who acted as muscle donors without benefit of anaesthetics. Although Aryan blood was never to be mixed through intermarriage with non-Aryans, it was quite acceptable that sub-human organs could be used to save the life of a member of the master race.

Soviet commissars who were Jewish had to be captured alive, photographed, measured, questioned on their ancestry, then killed. Their skulls were despatched to Doctor Hirt at Strasbourg's medical faculty. Gradually his demands outgrew supplies and he then required the entire skeleton, and why not have the body too, since it was easier to transport living victims than corpses without attracting attention. Prisoners were then gassed with cyanide only on arrival, and still-warm bodies were laid on the good doctor's operating table.

Regretfully, the allied victory put an end to these experiments, just as they might have led to discoveries which would have changed the fate of humanity and improved our lot. At the same time, it put a temporary stop to the final solution's implementation, just as its beneficent effect was being felt. This was a great mistake. Such an operation should not stop half way, as General Amin once remarked. It could have prevented all the bloodshed that has since happened in the middle-east, as Israel would not have existed. The return of the Cold War would have been avoided, international relations would not have been jeopardised, and what for? Just some vague idea of being humanitarian, when only six million Jews had died! Some will say that the whole thing has to start again from scratch, and that soon.

*   *   *

So, be it rape or torture, intensive bombing or pillage, genocide or little local massacres, every available means of killing can be justified in the end, even though the reasoning may seem obscure.

Better still: the most extreme measures, the bloodiest combat tactics, the most appalling acts are finally the kindest, for the good reason that they hasten the end of hostilities, thus reducing the number of people killed and equipment lost. The famous Marshal Hindenburg defended this point of view when he said: "The more merciless is war, the more humane in reality, since it will end more quickly." This remains today's thinking among our finest strategists.

President Truman decided to drop the atom bomb on Japan after studying potential losses by America if her troops had invaded by sea. These losses were thought to amount to at least 300,000 men. The atom bomb was calculated to cost only 150,000 lives — all of them Japanese. There was no need to hesitate.

Logically, any new major conflict involving nuclear capability, would lend itself to the theory that a surprise attack which wiped out some three million people in a few seconds, would avoid dragging out the conflict and save many precious lives.

Chapter 4
Gods of War

Our ancestors in their animal skins shook with fright every time they heard thunder. Not understanding where it came from, they made it into a god. Some of their descendants took their cue from this example. As they found war confusing and mysterious, they decided that the only explanation possible had to be metaphysical. "War is sacred, instituted by God . . . God's will."[10]

Clearly, the sacred nature of war extends to all methods employed to wage it, detailed in the last chapter. Thus, not only are summary executions, massacres, and gratuitous cruelty useful to the authorities, but they are also made sacred by the fact that they originate from the conduct of a war. This is reassuring indeed. We can exterminate our fellows with a clear conscience — it is God's will.

All this is a heavy responsibility for the Almighty. He might have been allowed to share it, for instance with the Devil, who would naturally have received the worst share of it. And yet no — the Almighty has to take on the entire burden, the good as well as the bad being laid at His door, defeat as well as victory, acts of bravery as well as appalling butcheries. Man has washed his hands of it all.

This is a very practical point of view, as it means that on the one hand man accepts no responsibility for the conflicts which have torn the world apart since it began, and on the other hand he has taken to himself with great delight the role of God's instrument with its ensuing honours. Indeed a leader of men in the past was often a religious leader too. Such was the case among Roman generals, Aztecs, Japanese emperors, and Czars of Russia, who were both army chiefs and heads of the orthodox church. Some diehards still exist, such as the sovereign of Great Britain.

This intermingling of warring and religious functions stems from the personalities of the gods who were always great warriors in ancient creeds. The Scythians held Tivus to be the greatest god because of his athleticism which enabled him to preside over every battle. Assyrian gods were fearful combatants, revelling in luxury, surrounded by eunuchs and favourites. Examine them closely and you can see a disturbing resemblance to contemporary kings. In Graeco-Roman mythology, Mars awarded himself the title "killer of men". Pallas never left Olympus without his buckler and shield and his spear. Apollo always carried his quiverful of arrows; and Jupiter, with his thunderbolts, was the father of modern artillery.

With gods belonging one and all to the armed forces, it seemed natural that they should favour their comrades-in-arms when these came a cropper. Hence the paradise which they created, and which is nothing less than an armed services club, full members only, with the best seats reserved for old soldiers who had shown the greatest bravery on the field of battle. For example, a Fiji islander's ghost would have to prove that he had carried out a sufficient number of massacres and destroyed a certain number of villages. The river tribe from the gulf of Papua classified the dead according to their merit as combatants: those who fell in battle at the top, then warriors who did not meet their deaths on the battlefield, and bottom of the list, the little people unlucky enough to die in their own beds. Among the Aztecs and Peruvians, only warriors are allowed access to the Paradise of the Sun; mere civilians are put in an obscure and unhealthy basement.

In the Scandinavian Valhalla, under the tender gaze of Odin, god of war, the elect, surrounded by trophies, slaves and prisoners, and served by glamorous Valkyries, drink milk and honey from the enemy's skulls, eat his cattle, share out his possessions, and joy of joys, for afters, are allowed to cut each other to pieces in the celestial palace's courtyard.

Brahmin India, home-to-be of Gandhi the pacifist, is enormously warlike. In the Vedas are countless descriptions of battles that go on forever; Hindu temples are covered in sculptures of gods battling it out with great delight in their chariots of war; and in Ramayana, Walnicki declares "the very earth drinks the blood of fallen warriors, and laughs through the open mouths of dying heroes."

With this quotation, we can hope to penetrate into a greater understanding of the tight link between war and religion. Indeed we may ask why it is that different cultures show gods to be warriors, and why military leaders have priestly duties.

The answer is to be found in the concept of sacrifice. War is a punishment inflicted on mankind to wash away our sins. What a large number of sins man must have committed, for them to be absorbed at such a price! What dreadful wrongs must we be responsible for, given such determined chastisement!

One might think that the disasters, bereavements, illnesses and disabilities which daily fall on us are sufficient penance. But no, there has not been enough suffering, not enough depth to it. We must have war to tip the balance. Oceans of blood are required. "Man must slaughter his fellows; the whole world, soaked in blood, is nothing less than one enormous altar ready to receive the ultimate sacrifice of everything that lives, without pause, without end until all is consumed." This chronic thirst for human blood, which afflicts the gods, leads them to make frequent demands, before, during and after a battle. Before it, a sacrifice of propitiation. A few lads are slaughtered to appease the gods and ensure their protection. During the battle, a warrior is in turn priest at the altar and victim. As priest, he must strike with knife and gun, kill all around him. Then comes the moment when he too falls, and becomes the willing victim. The sacrifice is complete.

After the battle, and if victory has rewarded the warriors' ardour, the sacrifice takes the form of a thanksgiving, to pay homage for the gods' generous intervention, presents are offered. Note in passing that such gifts are worth more in the eyes of the divinities because they create more suffering among those offering them up. Giving up part of the spoils to place them at the foot of the altar is no great effort. Cutting short the life of a few sheep is already better, since the taking of life is good in the eyes of our Maker. But the divine palate has a preference for the taste of human flesh rather than mutton. And so, in the general emphasis of victory, a few thousand souls will be sacrificed, or even ten or twenty thousand, for thrift is not the order of the day and in any event they will usually be prisoners of war.

Hence war does not appear to us to be a symbol, a mere image, but a real sacrifice, of some style, and indeed it could be argued that war is the ultimate sacrifice, where entire nations offer up their life's blood for the delectation and gratification of protective deities. Screams of tortured beings, moans of the wounded and death rattles of the dying, sound to their ears like celestial music. The stench of blood, the nauseous breath of dying men, the stink of corpses waft to their august nostrils like precious incense.

It is to be noted too that much as the Almighty is pleased at the immolation of large numbers of human beings, his pleasure is of a subtler kind if the sacrifice is required of people that are particularly dear to Him. What was required of Abraham to prove his devotion? That he should strike down his own son. In the same way, the leader will send his best boys against the toughest opponents. To put into the front line the ailing, the arthritic, the rejects — what an insult to the Almighty! Chiefs must choose the young, the strong, those full of promise. Should he send them to certain death, then indeed will he attain to the sublime, for the more he requires of his men, the greater he becomes, until he is almost divine. Great generals expect more — kill another ten thousand at once. Debonnaire kings and captains without a massacre to their name remain obscure and laughable characters. When Hitler sent a telegram to his cherished youth, though, to his 300,000 soldiers at Stalingrad, flower of the German army, telling them to stand and die, no-one laughed.

For their part, soldiers grow increasingly attached to a leader whose demands are great. They are ready to run to their deaths. All they need to know is that God is with them. For a long time now, leaders of men have known the art of persuading simple soldiers that they are God's right arm, and that He has given them the task which they are to accomplish. To fight for God has more merit than to fight for oil, and as the philosopher Joseph de Maistre points out, men are condemned to die anyway, so a few years here or there — what difference does it make?

*   *   *

It is time now to knock on the head a widespread fallacy, namely that Christianity, as opposed to other religions, is pacifist by nature.

In the first place, we have to note that it is not for nothing that our civilisation bears the name Judeo-Christian. Catholic, Orthodox and Protestant religions emanate directly from the Jewish religious tradition and the New Testament is the spiritual heir of the Old. What then does the latter have to say about war?

"For by fire will the Lord execute judgement, and by his

sword upon all flesh . . . And you shall destroy all the peoples
that the Lord your God will give over to you, your eye shall not
pity them . . . O daughter of Babylon, you devastator! Happy
shall he be who requites you with what you have done to us!
Happy shall he be who takes your little ones and dashes them
against the rock!"

The God of armies calls on his troops to go into training.

> Prepare for war,
> stir up the mighty men.
> Let all the men of war draw near,
> let them come up.
> Beat your ploughshares into swords,
> and your pruning-hooks into spears . . .

Much Hebrew history is full of wars, assassinations, rapes and
ravages. The Chosen People fought against the Assyrians, the
Egyptians, the Ethiopians, then the two kingdoms — Israel and
Judah — battled it out, and there were even a number of
fratricidal wars between the ten tribes. The Almighty thunders,
bellows, strikes his beloved people with famine, and allows its
women with nothing else to eat to sample their children. Nor is
He any kinder to the enemies of Israel, whom He does not
hesitate to wipe out, to break like the potter's vessel, to drown in
the Red Sea, or to strike with lightning from the hands of his
Archangel. Gentle King David cries out:

> I pursued my enemies and overtook them,
> and did not turn back till they were consumed.
> I thrust them through, so that they were not able to
>   rise;
> they fell under my feet.

The Lord gives military leaders very precise instructions: you
must burn every enemy chariot, hamstring the horses, cut down
trees, dam rivers, lay waste fields with rocks and boulders,
pillage towns and set them alight, and do away with all living
creatures. "Put all menfolk to the sword, and their women too.
Show mercy only to virgins, for they are given over to you."[12]
The Almighty does not go in for half measures.

*   *   *

Let us move on to the New Testament. There is no doubt that
here and there a few unfortunate phrases do crop up, such as:
"Love your enemies, and pray for those who persecute you . . .

be at peace with one another . . . Peace on earth to men of good will." The first Christians, simple men, took these injunctions seriously and believed in good faith that Christ was offering them a revolutionary doctrine involving forgiveness for trespasses, love of our neighbour and turning the other cheek. They even managed to find in ancient Jewish scriptures isolated phrases with a similar message, or so they thought, such as: "You shall not kill. One name of God is Peace, love peace and work for peace." A scandalous development: ecclesiastical dignitaries coming straight out with a condemnation of war. Saint Ambrose saying: "To spill a man's blood, even in time of war, is to destroy God's creation." Origen believing that "the military profession is not suitable for a Christian. Christians fight only with prayer, and wars are invariably made by devils." Tertullian making the point that "true Christians cannot be soldiers, because being a soldier means killing and Christians cannot do that." Or Saint Basil condemning: "War is contrary to justice."

These trifles were dangerous. Initially persecuted, the Church was growing in strength and influence. Christians themselves will admit in all honesty that "the weak use different weapons from the strong . . . The young Church was weak and had to submit to violence against her, but once God had made her strong, why should she not take advantage of it?"[13] The Church was becoming a power in the land. She must adopt a realistic attitude.

This was the moment when Saint Augustine made his entrance. This fiery theologian understood at once that the Church had to deal with another power, the state, and that she could not forever take a high-and-mighty attitude, but must go into the bear garden of politics, temporal interests and battles.

Saint Paul had already opened up this road by stating that "there is no authority except from God, and those authorities that exist have been instituted by God. Therefore he who resists the authorities resists what God has appointed." Saint Augustine widened the breach. So as not to sin, he argued, it is enough not to want war for war's sake, but only for the peace it will bring. War waged for a just cause is legitimate, and God will reward us for it, as soldiers obey His instructions and take up arms to defend the divine order. "If God, by a special instruction, gives the order to kill, then homicide becomes a virtuous act . . . a soldier's profession is rewarding, honest and pleasing to God."[14] This doctrine is officially adopted by the Church from that time on. The die is cast. The Reformation will make little difference. Luther reminds us that "It is not man, but God, who hangs, beheads, breaks bones, slaughters and wages war." Cromwell will say to his men: "Trust in God, and keep your powder dry." With consciences as pure as new-born babes, Christians will henceforward slay all those who stand in their way, either because of their influence, or their wealth or their refusal to think the same way, for monotheism is by nature intolerant. Numerous pagan gods of ancient religions welcomed gods of conquered nations with open arms, but Allah or Jehovah is a jealous God. Not for Him a share of prayer and sacrifice. There is room only for one God. The real one, of course. And for only one religion. Others must disappear. Co-existence of a number of religions within one state seemed to our ancestors as incongruous as the idea of two governments would seem to us today, which shows how much religious life was integrated into the political life of a nation.

For a single religion to be established, the first necessity which comes to mind is the enforced conversion of all wrong-thinking people. Methods to be employed to this end, separately, in succession or simultaneously are persuasion and violence. A Christian soldier begins by showing pagans the advantages of his convictions, the strong points of his doctrine, and the spiritual security it brings him. But all too soon he will run out of arguments, as it is not easy to express the inexpressible. You cannot sell an unfathomable mystery like a hoover. You believe in it or you do not. If the customer remains unconvinced, asks awkward questions, argues and quibbles, then the Christian soldier has to become more soldier than Christian, and instead of talking, take action. This is known as persuasion by force, or conversion by the sword.

It sometimes happens that agnostics or heretics, tougher than expected, stubbornly refuse to be converted. Saint Thomas Aquinas admits that the only choice left is death. It is the most generous way to deal with infidels. Rather than cruelly leaving them to a lifetime of feeling their way in the darkness of unbelief, they are despatched to outer darkness. No need for remorse, especially in the case of primitive or so-called primitive peoples. As one missionary explained, since God has not redeemed their souls with His blood, "we must make no distinction between them and the basest animals."[15]

Man learns to kill in the name of his Maker. Crusades are launched against Turks, heretics, Lutherans, Anabaptists. Saint Bernard's cry is taken up: "Woe to him whose sword does not taste blood!" And that too of Arnould, abbot of Citeaux and papal legate: "O sword, leap from the scabbard, sharpen yourself and shine forth to maim and to slaughter!" Muslims are to be massacred, Jews to be burnt, pagans to be hanged, all in the purest spirit of Christian chivalry.

In the great days of yore, faith was strong, religion thrived, Popes were not afraid to exchange their cassocks for a breastplate, kings had to swear as part of their coronation ceremony to exterminate all heretics, and the great minister Bossuet congratulated Louis XIV for following this wise tradition, telling him: "This will be the greatest task of your reign." The ecclesiastical authorities were charged with the constant care of preserving a link between the Church and the Army.

This spiritual alliance needed a solid philosophical base, and skilled interpreters have analysed with the right emphasis the most delicate passages of the Gospels, especially the Sermon on the Mount, practically a Christian charter in which Jesus sets out the eight beatitudes, of which the seventh emphasises: "Blessed are the peacemakers, for they will be called Sons of God." Theologians put forward an initial premise, that this may be a reverse meaning, such as is found in the name Pacific Ocean, so called because it is particularly violent. A slightly less bold interpretation is that it may be the result of poor translation of the Hebrew word shalom, which via the Greek and the Latin may have lost its original sense of inner peace, of calm and serenity. The real meaning of the sentence would then be: "Blessed be those whose souls are at peace, for they will be called Sons of God."

There is another point of view. The Sermon on the Mount should be interpreted 'spiritually' and not literally. It is a rule for one's inner life, an ideal. Christ's commandments should not be considered as tablets of stone, but as guidelines. Moreover, these principles as they have come down to us, are linked to a limited historical horizon, which undermines their practical value.

It could also be argued that they are not meant for this world, but for God's kingdom to come, which means that we have plenty of time to come to terms with them.

Let us now deal with the following disastrous statement, also to be found in the Sermon on the Mount: "You have heard that it was said, 'You shall love your neighbour and hate your enemy.' But I say to you, Love your enemies and pray for those who persecute you." Thomas Birt's interpretation is cunning. This theologian maintains that Jesus' advice only applies to man individually. That particular man has to be loved, even if everything pushes you to hating him. On the other hand it is permissible and even recommended that you should hate and fight a collective enemy. Abbot Giran, one of the most inspired commentators on the Bible, states that: "These four verses . . . have no relevance to the use of brute force . . . or to the question of armaments and war" and it would be "damaging to their meaning to make them the absolute rule for human relations, as Tolstoy wanted to do."

The abbot then refers to the centurion who asked Jesus to cure his servant. He notes that the Master made no indictment of his interlocutor's profession; on the contrary, he gives this officer as an example of rectitude to the crowds surrounding him. What other conclusion can there be but Abbot Giran's, that Jesus supports the whole concept of armed forces? Furthermore, is there not a remarkable parallel between the Son of Man and a soldier? The former suffered and gave his life to save the world. The latter suffers and gives his life to save his country. Christians who obey the Nazarene's call, leaving behind their families, their lands and their homes, are no different from conscripts who depart for the front, leaving behind their kin and their possessions. Lastly, the Master who watches so that no thief may enter his house, is surely the sentry who keeps watch and is always ready for war.

There is one incident, just when Jesus is arrested, and one of his disciples "stretched out his hand and drew his sword, and struck the sleeve of the high priest, and cut off his ear. Then Jesus said to him, 'Put your sword back into its place; for all who take the sword will perish by the sword'." But the Abbot makes the point that this last comment is only to be found in Matthew. So why have the other Apostles not quoted it? It is tempting to conclude that the statement was not authentic. It could have been a subsequent addition which was meant to qualify a rather militaristic passage in the original text. Christian communities, three or four generations in, lived dangerous lives. An incident involving an ear cut off was compromising, with its touch of revolt. Hence the qualifying phrase inserted by the man responsible for the final edition, and which was never actually spoken.

We are at one with Abbot Giran that Christ's message is a call to armed resistance, and that far from disapproving of the use of weapons, he recommends it and even demands it. As the Abbot says: "He who takes up the sword of deliverance, as Jesus tells us to do, becomes by his action, the weapon of God."

Anxious Christian souls, supposing there are any at this joyful opening of the 20th century, can stifle their scruples without fear. By a happy coincidence the Great War with Germany will mobilise French and English ecclesiastical opinion. Already, some padres have made use of their colonial military experience to try out their militant form of religion. On 17 April 1896 in a Paris church, Father François Ollivier gives a brilliant sermon at a memorial service for the French killed in the fighting in Madagascar. (It is hardly necessary to make the point that there is no need to mention the thousands who died on the other side in defence of their lands.)

"France," says the Reverend, "does not believe . . . that civilisation can penetrate to the very heart of barbarism and remain there, merely through contacts created by commerce and industry. Nor does she believe this can be achieved by a certain philosophy . . . She may not even accept that the spread of the Apostolate will achieve it. She has no choice but to wage war to bring about a conversion to her own form of civilisation, not so much for her own gain, but for the benefit of those she conquers."

1905. Wilhelm II lands in Tangier. 1911. The German battleship 'Panther' drops anchor in front of Agadir. War clouds loom over the horizon. In all the churches of Europe priests let loose a barrage of words, firing off in every direction, electrifying the faithful, who, while remaining safely at home, are overcome with war fever and declare themselves ready and willing to make the supreme sacrifice — persuading the mass of insignificant little people to stumble into the slaughter-houses of glory and honour.

The Catholic hierarchy does what it can to prepare men's souls for military service, with a slight adjustment to Jesus' message: "thou shalt not kill" becomes "thou shalt not kill without due justification." The stage is set for the grand opening of August, 1914, and at last, all nations will have a role in the bloodbath.

Benedict XV, a good man, did become a little concerned, but how could his faltering appeals for peace withstand the front line of militant bishops? He tried, with timid words: "May the man who first lifts up the olive branch of peace and extends the hand of friendship to his enemy be blessed."

To which the archbishop of Lyons replied: "This is a war which every Frenchman must and wants to wage."

The Holy Father's feeble entreaties find no support on the other side. One German prelate explains: "A soldier is given cold steel to use without fear. He must plunge it into his enemy's body. He must break his rifle on their skulls. That is his sacred duty, his duty to God."

1918. Soldiers have understood and done their sacred duty. They have plunged cold steel into bodies and broken rifle butts on skulls. The mess is at an end, and the candles are blown out. As for the eight million dead, one priest points out with persuasive skill that if they had lived, theirs would probably have been lives with little moral significance, even less spiritual achievement, possibly ending without dignity, and all in all, uselessly. How lucky they were to avoid that.

There was just a chance that the Church might have taken a wrong turning between the First and Second World Wars, closing its mind to military requirements. But the threat was never real. Everything seems to be ready and the participants have only to wait. They will not have to wait long.

As soon as war breaks out, so does a moving chorus of episcopal appeals for discipline, acceptance and obedience. "Dearly beloved . . . submit yourselves absolutely to the regulations", orders the bishop of Algiers.

At the same time, the bishops guarantee that as always God is on our side. "We are strong, the Almighty is with us. He will give us victory . . ."[16]

Alas! The Allies, archbishops and bishops had been a little previous. God was not on our side. Probably He had other things to do in May 1940. Never mind. No hesitation from the gentlemen of the Church, who very quickly turn their coats. "We must rally round the great Marshal Petain, without hesitation", is the cool decree of the archbishop of Aix. Cardinal Baudrillant congratulates young Frenchmen who have donned the uniform of the Wermacht and sworn to obey the Fuhrer. They "are playing their part in the great renaissance of our country."

The same loyalty can be found at the heart of the Third Reich, which should not be unduly surprising since close links had existed for some years between the Catholic Church and the National-Socialists.

It must be recalled that a Concordat had been signed by Rome and Berlin in 1933, on the initiative of von Papen, to whom Chancellor Hitler largely owed his ascension to power. Von Papen's dream was to re-establish the Germanic Holy Roman Empire under the symbols of the Eagle and the Cross, and stretching from the Alps to the Urals. This Concordat "gave the National-Socialist authority, generally considered to be a government of usurpers or even of ruffians, the cachet of an accord with the most ancient international power, whose authority spread far beyond the Catholic world. It was rather like receiving an international award of respectability."[17] Von Papen might well be proud of his success. One of his sayings was that "the Third Reich is the first world power not just to have recognised the exalted principles of the Papacy, but to have put them into practice." Now he had ensured a lasting collaboration between the Church and the German High Command which never ceased throughout the war, despite some minor difficulties — certain ecclesiastical goods confiscated a shade brutally, large numbers of monasteries closed rather tactlessly, attempts to make some turbulent bishops see the error of their ways, deportation or beheading of a few dozen priests. Such peccadilloes cannot stand in the way of necessities of state.

On the whole, the Nazi leaders were members of the Catholic tradition. Himmler belonged to a leading Catholic family: his father had been head of a Catholic school in Munich, his uncle was a Jesuit and a Canon of the Church, he had a brother who was a Benedictine monk, and he had close contacts of his own with the Jesuit General Fr. Ledochowski. Goebbels, the indefatigable minister of Propaganda, had been brought up by the Jesuits, and had considered joining their order before he rallied to the New Order. The family of Rudolph Hess was fanatically pious. The Führer himself benefited from a religious education. In Rausching's biography, Hitler declares: "I learnt most of all from the order of Jesuits . . . Until now, there has been nothing to equal the grandeur of the Catholic Church on earth, with its hierarchical organisation. I have transferred a major part of this organisation to my own party."

War came, and found the temporal and spiritual powers "hand in hand for the reform of the world", in the words of Monsignor Tiso, head of the Slovak state. He practised what he preached: after getting his hand in with a number of influential members of the Protestant Church, he sent off — with his apostolic benediction — the very first contingent of Jews to Auschwitz, in the year of grace 1941. This goodly priest, who was always saying how Slovakia would be "governed along Christian lines", was apparently much liked by the Holy See. Everyone can make a mistake, even in Rome. No-one expected that Mgr. Tiso would end up hanged come the Liberation.

The pious governor of West Bosnia, Victor Cutic, did not lag behind his neighbour with his own vision of a Christian mission. "I have taken draconian measures to annihilate the Serbs, and the New Order will result. We must show them no mercy. We must be pitiless . . . Slaughter them wherever you see them, and you will be blessed . . . I must bow to God's will."

Large numbers of clerical dignitaries join in the hunt, carried away by the ardour of these champions of evangelical charity, sounding their horns in the cathedrals, crying that "Germany's war is Christianity's war". The German Ministry of Ecclesiastical Affairs, not backward in coming forward, is quite happy to add a paragraph to the accepted doctrine relating to the Trinity. In an outburst of patriotic mysticism, it declares: "Just as Christ brought together his twelve disciples, men faithful to the point of martyrdom, so are we witnessing the same events today. Indeed, Adolf Hitler has become the Holy Spirit."

As soon as the Holy Spirit had taken on this unexpected form, how could the clergy not have made full use of this miraculous manifestation to bring together the scattered flock of the faithful? How could the churches not be full to bursting? How could we not see banners of the Virgin Mary and standards bearing the swastika side by fraternal side, under the soaring domes?

It is important to understand that war particularly encourages a return to the ranks of the faithful under the influence of a religious authority. When war breaks out, the Church benefits in every country. "There is nothing like shared suffering and constant danger at hand, to bring men back to the caring arms of God.''[18] A silver lining — people hurry to church, pilgrimages are booked up, and those who minister this new cult become zealous again, frantically converting lost souls, like a new crusade. Fear of death is a good counsellor. "When machine-guns speak, childhood prayers return."[19]

In turn, the military owe a good deal to religion. "A warrior who does not put his trust in God has no strength, no courage, no power." He is a complete weakling "if God does not dwell in his mind to encourage him . . . what is more, should a soldier forget God while he lives, he must remember Him in death. What more eloquent and spiritual temple can there be than a battlefield?" Headquarters know this: "Men of God are the very best adjutants to military leaders, because their holy doctrine urges them to bring out all that is patriotic and heroic in a soldier's soul."[20]

Have the clergy gone too far in aiding and abetting military authorities? Has the Church, totally absorbed by political and strategic objectives, rather neglected spiritual values? Has the Vatican, protector of the Gospels with their message of tolerance, generosity, love of one's neighbour, shut its eyes on certain regrettable acts of violence, especially the way the direct descendants of Jesus and his disciples were treated? Or must we believe that the Holy See knew nothing at all about persecution, death camps and gas chambers?

The latter was Pope Pius XII's explanation during an interview with Dr. Nerim Gun, correspondent with the *Gazette de Lausanne*, on 15 November 1945. "We were never told about the inhuman conduct of the Nazi repression." The journalist insists: "How could your Holiness's representatives in Germany have kept this from you?" — "The information they had was incomplete and it was difficult for them to communicate it to us."

And yet . . . Some testimonies seem to contradict the Holy Father. Men worthy of trust say that the Vatican has always been "one of the most efficient centres of information in the world" simply because "all its priests are de facto agents working for the Vatican, and its ambassadors have access to methods of obtaining information not available to other diplomats."[21] Pius XII's biographer and admirer, Fr. Duclos, has to admit that "thanks to his unique network of information centres", the head of the Church is "best placed to assess particular cases from a truly universal point of view." Camille Cianfarra, *New*

York Times Vatican correspondent, and a man who could
hardly be suspected of vilifying the Pope, put much the same
argument, and says that "the Vatican never ceased being
remarkably well informed of the internal situation in Europe's
various nations ... Priests serving both tiny country parishes
and major urban ones, passed regular reports on to their
diocesan bishops, and one way or another these reports always
ended up in Rome." Finally, a regular presenter on Vatican
Radio, Fr. Mistiaen, said of his German colleagues: "One of
them, who obtained his information first hand, brought me the
most damning documents relating to the inhuman cruelty of
the Nazis in Poland."

Must we conclude that Pius XII, in his reply to Dr. Gun, was
not entirely honest? The truth is more subtle. In fact, the Pope
was fully informed, but how could he have admitted it, *urbi et
orbi*, without irretrievable damage to that famous ecclesiastical
discretion? As Fr. Duclos wrote: "Too direct a condemnation, in
language too clearly understood, presents a triple danger: being
wrong, increasing the amount of persecution already occurring,
and damaging the interests of the Church and humanity."

As far as clear language was concerned, that was safely in the
hands of the Papal writers. The Third Reich's ambassador to the
Holy See, Von Weizsäcker, makes an interesting witness, writing
in a private memorandum: "The Pope, though under pressure
from every side, refused to condemn publicly the deportation of
Jews from Rome ... He did everything he could in this delicate
matter not to jeopardise relations with the German government
and German aides in Rome."

Weizsäcker goes on to discuss a Papal communiqué published
by l'Osservatore Romano on 25th–26th October 1943 which he
says "is couched in Vaticanese, that is, in a contorted and vague
style, stating that the Pope looks after the interests of all men,
without distinction of nationality, race, or religion, and cares for
them paternally ... There is all the more reason for not
objecting to this message, since few people will recognise he is
referring specifically to the Jewish question."

This is the art of making a point without appearing to do so,
and yet making it all the while.

Only on 2nd June 1945, a month after Germany has been
crushed, does Pius XII come out with the tough condemnation
so long awaited, with the words: "the Satanic evil that was
National-Socialism."

Better late than never.

*   *   *

The Church has suffered a regrettable revolution under the influence of left-wing priests recently. The abandoning of Latin, which had enabled the faithful to mumble their prayers without understanding a word, their thoughts elsewhere, and an increasingly familiar attitude to God in the faithful's prayers, all this has helped the clergy, including very senior ecclesiasts, to express subversive opinions with impunity.

Defeatism and pacifism appeared to be stemming from the very centre of the Church. John XXIII's inspiration, Vatican II, did not hesitate to break with the tradition set down by St. Augustine, or to condemn the arms race, or to hope that "we would free ourselves from the ancient servitude of war". Paul VI forgot himself to the point of saying: "Peace is possible, if all of us want it, if we all love it . . . defend it, work towards it." Terrible words, for the supreme head of the Church.

Unworthy prelates began a wicked campaign to undermine systematically the value of nuclear arms. The bishop of Orleans put his foot in it just a few days before France tested a nuclear bomb on Mururoa atoll on 10th July 1973. He maintained in a press statement that "no political or economic interests of any nation can justify the use of the Bomb . . . All French people anxious about a peaceful future must demonstrate their disapproval as clearly as possible."

The political world was astonished, totally lost for words. Such a thing had never been seen. A cleric, setting himself up against the establishment! A man of the cloth against the armed forces! Something must be done. The French Ambassador to the United States made the most of Bastille-day celebrations on 14th July to launch a counter-attack. The episcopal proposals were, to him, "the desperate ramblings of unsound minds". The then Prime Minister of France, Pierre Messmer, reminded us that "never in history has the Church succeeded when she meddled with questions of armament." One general, who probably rated women very badly, lashed out against what he described as "moralising pacifism with a distinctly female touch." Churchmen representing the armed forces declared that a balance of power held through terror is as good as any other. But the conclusive point was made by Admiral de

Joybert, naval chief of staff — nor did he mince his words. "People whose only profession, and what a noble one, is to care for our souls, tend to talk absolute nonsense when they interfere with military matters. That will do, gentlemen of the priesthood, would you please mind your own business!"

The old sea-dog had fired his broadside. He earned our congratulations and deserves our support. Quite ridiculous to think that the Church should busy itself with anything more than the question of church-cleaning rosters and the height of candles on the altar. Why should she have her say on such questions as how men live, suffer, work; the situation for immigrants, unemployed, juvenile delinquents, or the question of property speculation. Why should she make the rich anxious with fairy stories like the one about a camel going through the eye of a needle more easily than a rich man entering heaven? The last thing we want is for the Church to poke its nose about, where there are massacres, mass violence, acts of injustice, torture and war. Where would that lead us?

Rest assured, Admiral. The still small voice of the long-haired hippie, who 2,000 years ago proclaimed unwanted and disconcerting truths from the wilderness, urging us to love one another — for many years now this small voice has been drowned by bombs, sermons and guns.

Chapter5
Panacea

Sooner or later a nation, just like any other living organism, will feel the need to expand. This can only be done through military conquest. It would be unbecoming for two countries to decide to join together at the request of international agencies, or worse still, at their own behest, freely expressed, following consultation of their own citizens.

Conquest, on the other hand, is accepted by philosophers and law-makers. It is normal, necessary, "the most legitimate action possible, a natural method of acquiring new land."[22] It lies in an ancient and well established tradition. The Romans believed that a conquering army should naturally take possession of land, towns and inhabitants. Richelieu saw no difference between conquest through violence and Christian charity, as long as it was done by the book. Building an empire can be seen as a duty "if a great nation appears to be heading for ruin unless it pushes out its frontiers." One could go further and claim "that a head of state who shows mercy to his fallen enemy rather than cold-bloodedly pursuing the best interests of his own country, is guilty of betraying it and must be condemned on a moral level."[23] Monarchs have made considerable use of military conquest to enlarge and secure their kingdoms, but that does not mean that government through monarchy is any more warlike than other systems. There is no doubt that our goodly kings enjoyed making war more than any other pastime, but numbered among the most warlike nations have been the Roman, Venetian and Swiss republics. Historians agree today that the aggression of states has nothing to do with their political persuasions.

Military conquest — legitimate, normal and sometimes necessary though it may be — is often involuntary. The future conqueror may have no plan in his head at all when he opens hostilities. No premeditation whatsoever. Suddenly he is victorious, his enemy at his mercy. Will he help himself to a chunk of his land? It is very tempting. First, he talks about a few minor concessions, one or two towns, a narrow band of territory. But the more he takes, the more he wants. The next suggestion is for a larger piece of land — half a province, say. By the utmost coincidence, the portion he takes contains mines, uranium deposits or oil wells. In any event, he has plenty of reasons for his actions — it is his duty to ensure future security, to guard against counter-attacks; and surely he is entitled to levy payments to cover the damages done in war? Many of these damages will naturally have been suffered by the vanquished nation rather than the conqueror, but the former lost, so he pays.

Imperceptibly, then, war becomes conquest. War breaks out to save Danzig and preserve Poland's independence. But the war grows, takes over four continents, and the original cause is forgotten now that other aims have appeared.

The year is 1943 — who remembers Danzig? There are other problems to be dealt with, one after another. Once the Nazis have been defeated, the influence of the Soviets increases. Japan beaten, China wakes up. Power struggles ensue. Yesterday's requirements have been left behind. The bomb destroys not just Hiroshima, but contemporary strategy for our entire planet. Is it so surprising that the ambition of independence for Poland, the cause for which so many lost their lives, should have become redundant?

Some people maintain that military conquests do not last. They point to the glorious episodes of the Persians and Tamberlaine and argue that nothing is left. They say that Charles V's ambition led him from initial victories into defeat after defeat until he ended his days behind the grille of a monastery door. That military leaders everywhere, whose exploits we hear about endlessly, were eventually responsible for total fiascos. That Adolf Hitler, having conquered three-quarters of Europe, saw his dream shattered, his army crushed, his country defeated, and German unity, so patiently created by Bismarck, broken asunder for a very long time. Finally, that the colonies of the west, acquired after long and costly wars, threw off the yoke of the ruling power at the first opportunity.

It has to be admitted that military conquests do not always yield the expected result, and that certain disadvantages do exist. People whose houses have been occupied are hardly likely to feel warmly disposed to the conquering forces. They may make life difficult, and that is understandable. They will suffer, and who accepts suffering readily?

This means a certain amount of ill will. Little attention will be paid to rules and regulations drawn up by the invader. Deep hostility to him will appear in every gesture, in people's attitudes. There will be complaints and recriminations, followed by acts of sabotage, forcing the invader to act more severely. Repression will, in turn, invite resistance. Bombings ensue — a shop, a pub, a bus, a cinema. Blood flows. Those responsible are punished, if they are found. They are dubbed terrorists, and even if they were not before, they become so now. More incidents occur, reprisals increase in severity. This is the escalation of violence.

It is hard to avoid. The conquering nation would have to win the hearts and minds of the vanquished through a determined campaign. They would have to be loyal and true, tolerant and imaginative — qualities which, to be honest, tend to be rare among victorious peoples. They would have to avoid exploiting, impoverishing and starving their victims; appeal to their good sense; demonstrate the advantages of common sharing of resources and efforts. In other words, they would have to create a partnership, a full working relationship with a real alliance.

But if this is to be the end result, a 'lasting peace', as is constantly proclaimed, why not avoid the trouble of a war in the first place and sit down round a table without delay to open negotiations aimed at reaching a compromise?

How little do those making such a suggestion understand of human nature, and how lightly do they treat national pride. They have not taken into account a fundamental difference between a peaceful solution to conflict, and the same solution reached only after a devastating war. That difference is a few thousand, or a few hundred thousand, or even a few million dead.

That in a nutshell is the problem. Napoleon best perceived its significance when he wrote to Archduke Charles in his own brilliant style: "We shall kill . . . and eventually we will come to an agreement."

* * *

The philosopher Montaigne suspected that the Romans had "deliberately sought war with their enemies in order to satisfy their army's appetite for battle." Kings anxious about keeping

troops happy were advised "to find them a nice fat war, well
organised and justified. They will be satisfied, since men-at-
arms must not take their ease."

An army should not remain inactive for too long; bad habits
ensue. Men get rusty. To keep them in top condition, there is no
substitute for a real battle, risking life and limb. However well
drilled and equipped an army is, its commanding officer will
never be quite sure how it will perform in a real fight. It must
have an ordeal by fire. In the next chapter, we will study this
vicious circle more closely. A nation has an army prepared for
war, but a war is needed to prepare the army. It suffices for now
to note that soldiers cannot forever indulge in square-bashing.
There comes a point at the thousandth about-turn when
Tommy starts to wonder if someone is taking the mickey. There
is a limit to presenting arms without ever using them. Sooner or
later, he has to put what he has learnt into practice, and graduate
from war-game to war, using real bodies flowing with real
blood.

Waging war makes work for more than just the troops. It
enables the army to take on a large number of people who
would otherwise fill up the state's dole queues. It scoops up all
sorts of individuals, men without precise jobs, on the fringes of
society, without finance or cultural backgrounds, potentially
subversive or completely anti-social elements — all those who
in peace time would have no acceptable role in society, but who
can certainly join the army.

War enables the social climber to get on very fast. A loutish
private soldier ends up as Marshal of the Empire and acquires
his own crown to boot. Huang-Ti was a mercenary nobody,
before he became China's greatest emperor. Three-quarters of
Latin America and more than half the countries of black Africa
today have presidents who are also military leaders, as a well-
established tradition.

In European monarchies, the king always recompensed a
subject who had killed a decent number of people by giving him
some land, a title and privileges, which his son inherited, even if
he was a complete coward and had never been near a battle.
This practice created the original nobility. The other, com-
prising judges and other legal officers, never quite rivalled the
genuine aristocracy's prestige and splendour.

Nations specialising in trade have always envied their
militarily-inclined neighbours. Carthage had a 'sacred legion'

consisting of sons of leading bankers, merchants and ship-builders. In Venice, the offspring of the city's 'commercial aristocracy' always joined the army. In other monarchist countries, the black sheep sons of middle-class families did all they could to join up and become aristocrats by means of the sword. Many socialist nations today — Russia especially — boast sons of the Revolution covered in medals and resplendent in uniforms even though they spent their youth spitting on the uniforms of the previous regime's army.

This fascination for the army is not at all surprising if one remembers that war is actually at the very heart of all our social structures without exception. The division into social classes is not, as sociologists maintain all too frequently, the result of categorisation according to professional ability and qualifications, but the result instead of creating a race of slaves by taking prisoners, so that "conquering nations become the master race, and class divisions are born."[25]

The allocation of work is a direct consequence of war. "For men to rise above the level of animals, some of them have to be released from the all-embracing anxieties of hard work by others . . . Such a separation, of professional and working-class people never happened without coercion, and indeed was forced on strangers who were held to it against their will."[26] Differences of sex, age, needs and taste had no influence whatsoever on division of work. We owe to war the various functions which exist today, be it journalism, electronic engineering, architecture or whatever.

Man, left to his own devices, is naturally lazy. As soon as he has satisfied his basic needs, he stops working, he lies on the grass and looks at the trees and the sky. If he gets hungry, he goes in search of food. Then he returns to his dreaming. He has to be pushed, needled, constantly and without respite — by kicks in the pants if necessary — into a taste for work, for productivity increased by the sweat of his brow. He must be forced to squeeze onto rush-hour trains and buses, made to take exercise to keep fit — but war takes care of all that. Without it, he would probably die of starvation and boredom. Is it not infinitely better that he should die a violent death?

War goes further. It demands blind, unconditional, moronic obedience to one's sergeant, or captain, or general in order to teach men to revere their leaders and respect authority, the establishment, and lastly, the moral order. There is no doubt about it: war, which appears to violate every familiar ethical code (such as not committing murder, theft or extortion) is nevertheless seen by many philosophers as the inspiration and guarantor of virtue.

Most customs, traditions and practices have their origins in war. The philosopher Herbert Spencer has given us the best assessment of how what he calls 'ceremonial forms' originate with the military. Kissing hands, bowing, baring the head are relics of an attitude of submission to a conqueror.

Who would think that the ceremonial sword carried by a worthy knight of the garter today, is the same sword that a wretched warrior placed at the feet of his victorious enemy? Who would imagine too that an orchestra conductor's baton is the final transmutation of a warrior's lance, which underwent a number of metamorphoses, from lance to sceptre, symbol of power, to baton, symbol of authority?

The Jewish and Muslim practice of circumcision, according to Spencer, is directly derived from the practice of mutilation of conquered peoples, symbolising their enslavement by removing a part of the body. Sometimes mutilation is voluntary: to be well thought of by the victorious chief, a captive offers him a gift of some of his hair or part of an eyebrow. Gradually this custom becomes obligatory, and turns into a payment in a tribute or a levy. In other words, the taxman has his origins in military matters.

The custom of wearing clothes, according to Spencer, is not the result of protecting the body from bad weather or the need for decency. It stems from war. Clothing is needed as a distinctive sign of rank, of function, and eventually of class.

As for decorations, they are the leftover of trophies of battle and have the same significance as scalps, collections of skulls or ears proudly displayed by a chief to show his bravery. We accept that today they are mere symbols. These days no-one would literally walk about with his enemy's phallus displayed in his belt.

Spencer's idea is that all forms of ceremonial are the natural product of the relationship between the conqueror and his victim. The question must be asked: is there anywhere on this earth a custom, a greeting or badge which does not relate to military tradition?

*   *   *

Put yourself in the place of someone running the country, and it becomes evident that war is the most attractive diversion possible. As soon as internal problems become hard to handle, war with another state is the answer. Everything becomes so very simple: what only yesterday seemed disastrous and unresolvable, is simplified in a moment. Values change, priorities too. The older generation stops worrying that the younger will take its jobs, as the latter have found new employment more suitable to them on the field of battle. Incidents of delinquence drop suddenly. Why should they kill people on the streets now that special places have been reserved to allow anyone keen on murdering his fellow-man to go ahead? Unemployment, so feared, is just a bad memory; overnight, full employment is back, though no-one believed in it anymore. Even such secondary problems as traffic congestion and obesity find a solution, the first through petrol rationing, the second through food rationing.

The greatest changes occur surely in the political arena. No longer is it necessary to seek delicate compromises between opposing parties, to engage in finding a balance between divergent interests. Delicate or frankly embarrassing questions can be left to one side, to the relief of our leaders. No more elections, no more demands from the unions, no more protests; a censored Press, demonstrations forbidden, the opposition silenced. In the unlikely event that some pinprick of disagreement with the authorities should be felt, there is a magic and foolproof remedy, consisting of just a few words: public interest, restricted information, threat to the nation — and in extreme cases: collaboration with the enemy. Nothing can resist these charges.

This explains why the leader does not have to be particularly bright to govern, given all these methods of suppression, including the firing squad. With the army in support, everything will go smoothly, and gradually security forces will take over the reins of power. Often enough, nations have had completely incompetent kings or heads of state, thick in the head, quick to pass judgement, not to be contradicted, deaf to the advice of those around them, and convinced, in good faith or bad, that they have been chosen by divine right. Such idiots have sometimes held on to power during an entire war, even when it was obvious they were leading the nation into disaster.

Generally, men most hungry for honours, laurels and medals

pull themselves up to the top rank by their fingertips; which is why they often reveal themselves to be sadly childish. Alexander set fire to Persepolis to enjoy an extraordinary spectacle. As for **Napoleon, the day he learnt of Dupont's capitulation at Baylen,** he threw himself face down on the carpet, beating the floor with his fists, and sobbing for an hour. Whenever Hitler was crossed, he would scream and stamp his feet. Mussolini never grew bored with military parades, tank drive-pasts, flags to salute.

This love of vainglory is not restricted to generals and presidents, black or white. It is a bug which can affect clerks, shopkeepers, secretaries and curates. No-one is free from it. Perhaps the point is that we have a good idea as to our own mediocrity, and a need to compensate for this inferiority without taking any risks ourselves. Huxley explains: "Submissive to the wife, kind to the children, courteous to the neighbours, the soul of honesty in business, the good citizen feels a thrill of delight when his country 'takes a strong line', 'enhances its prestige', 'scores a diplomatic victory', 'increases its territory'."

The good citizen soon finds himself involved in a new and **extraordinarily fervent movement known as nationalism.** He will come to believe that his country is the best, the bravest, the fairest, the only one capable of defending the eternal values of culture, the rewards of civilisation, the highest interests of humanity. It will never cross his mind to doubt it. Whether he be British, French, German, Italian, Russian, Japanese or Zulu, he knows full well, deep inside, with no argument possible, that "Britain is predestined to transform the world",[27] that "only France has a right to be a nation",[28] that "America must remain the world's most powerful nation",[29] that "Germany's role is to protect and support European civilisation",[30] that "the only nation which has the right to exercise its claim to be paramount is the pre-eminently Catholic one, in other words Italy",[31] that "the Soviet people are guardians of the most advanced ideology and civilisation",[32] and that "the great Japan is superior to any other nation in the world".[33] Modest, too.

One way of persuading a good citizen of his own merit is to show him as simply as one and one make two, that the rest of the world is peopled with nothing but morons, lazy good-for-nothings, simpletons and pariahs. There is no difficulty, as this is just what he wants to hear, to be reassured. Anything with which he is unfamiliar frightens him, seems strange — hence **the use of the same word. He needs to exorcize his fear and the** way to do that is to imagine other people to be inferior human beings or even monsters. Fear becomes loathing, and xenophobia is born.

The enemy can then be described as "an untamed anthropoid with pink skin" whose face "bears the most terrible bestiality in its threatening and grotesque features", and is "aggressively ugly", whose hands are like "the huge hands of a strangler".[34] One can only have the "utmost loathing" for "cannibals" of that nature, "with never a hint of mercy, never deflecting from the goal of totally exterminating such a Satanic race . . . They must be treated with total contempt, with the purest, most perfect hatred."[35]

Animal instinct is at the root of human xenophobia. In the Far East, observers have noted that buffaloes cannot bear the smell of a white man, and they will attack a white as soon as he comes near them, whereas a yellow native will be unharmed. Were they able to speak, they would probably say that Europeans stink. The same thing happens among certain human beings, and this is nothing to do with logic, sociology or even reasoning. It is purely a neuro-psychological reaction. Some people cannot stand Arabs, so they beat them up a little, make them run the gauntlet. Others cannot bear the Jews, so they indulge in a few arrests, some persecution, a pogrom or two. Many people have a thing about blacks, unless the latter join the army where they become "great big children with good hearts full of daring and ready to give their all in exchange for the liberty we have offered them."[36]

The doctrine of racism was invented to give a fine name to this revulsion, which some people feel naturally for their fellowmen, so that it would not appear to be a bestial reaction.

The name may be recent, but the phenomenon is ancient. It was a belief in racial superiority which dictated the ancient world's system of slavery, as well as discrimination between original Christians and converts in 15th century Spain, or the use of blacks in America. The interesting development in nationalsocialism's racial doctrine is the scientific basis of the arguments put forward by Adolf Hitler and his leading theoretician, Alfred Rosenberg. Everything, they maintain, has been examined under the light of objective reasoning, and none of it involves subjective interpretations of history. They both stick to reliable proven and universally acknowledged facts.

Rosenberg, for instance, explains that "a blond and blue-eyed race ... its destiny known, a privileged people, once spread across the entire world" from a nordic centre of creation — Atlantis probably. Hitler goes on to explain how Aryan man, representing this superior race, created everything of note in our civilisation, thanks to the useful workforce he organised from among inferior races by overcoming them. He is "the Prometheus of the human race; and from time-immemorial a divine spark of genius has flashed from his glowing forehead." Unfortunately, he broke "a fundamental law": one which charges him to undertake the act of reproduction "only with a female of the same species — sparrow with sparrow, mouse with mouse, wolf with wolf." It could be argued that the author of *Mein Kampf* is mistaken, in that our species is said to be "a people made up of individuals able to reproduce themselves between any two of the opposite sex."[37] Man violates no fundamental law by coming together with other members of the same, human, species. But seen from the Nazis' point of view, anyone from an inferior race is not a human being, but an animal, a sub-human, in other words "the skeleton of man with roughly similar features, but spiritually and morally inferior to any animal."[38]

Science and racism come together satisfactorily. There is only one small problem, and that is the question of laws of genetics, which contradict absolutely any assumption that a pure race exists, and at the same time that there is such a thing as an inferior race, and the theory of degeneration through "mixed blood" is rubbish. Never mind! A few stirring phrases will obscure all that; Rosenberg writes: "The life of a race is not a logical development, but the result of a mystical synthesis." What is more, such "mystical vitality" is "cosmic" at the same time. "German man had cosmic solar sensations which allowed him to discover the eternal laws of the earth." Nothing could be clearer, and Hitler dotted the 'i's: to regenerate itself, the German race must do away with all inferior races which sully its purity as quickly as possible.

War will give men the opportunity to carry out a number of practical experiments.

*   *   *

These days, you can call yourself an atheist, a homosexual, a fascist, a naturist, an alchemist, or an anarchist in most liberal countries without any danger of going to prison or being beaten up. There is still one idol which you cannot throw stones at without being accused of blasphemy though, and that is patriotism.

Patriotism demands absolute devotion, which must be blind and fanatical. It takes precedence in all things. It needs no reason, brooks no disagreement — it is an article of faith, a consuming passion. Compared with this flame, "everything else, religion, political commitment, the social world, a profession, wealth, these are all secondary."[39] In today's society patriotism has become a cult, "love of country" has become "our religious impetus".[40] So much so that expressions of patriotism have taken on a liturgical style, like the wonderful remake of the Catholic credo for fascist Italian children. (See Appendix IV)

Patriotism smoulders in time of peace, but as soon as war looms, it bursts into flame. Nothing can stand in its way. Everyone — the timid, the half-hearted, the retiring sort, even those too busy scratching a living to be touched by the general conflagration — they all catch the collective fever. Old-style patriots find it sufficient to make ringing speeches, but for the new disciples, the movement carries them along and they will lay down their lives for their country. The irony of it all is that they really have nothing to defend, since they own nothing at all.

This patriotic wildfire sweeps away even those who only yesterday were screaming out their pacifism. The First World War taught us a significant lesson. Many Belgian, German, British, Russian and French socialists, who had poured scorn on the army and militarism, took a remarkable right turn as soon as war broke out. Various French writers spoke of "insurrection not war" one moment, and the "impudence of the Hun" the next; one author wrote: "not one penny to help the madness of war",[41] and shortly after he took a post in the War Cabinet; another wrote urging a general strike to "prepare for tough action"[42] against war, then he became minister responsible for armaments.

Such incredible enthusiasm, which is capable of provoking sudden conversions like the ones described does not seem to have been always the case as far as our ancestors are concerned. No-one knows quite when and how was born the concept which today is the keystone of our lives. But in the end, the origins of this patriotic sentiment hardly matter. It exists, and that is the main thing for us. Better still, it continues to grow in most of the 153 nations officially recognised by the United Nations. Such growth is evident in, say, the fanatical politico-religious emotions of the Middle-East, or an equal enthusiasm for politico-military matters in Africa and Asia. There is nothing more exciting than this absolute devotion to one's own people, government and institutions, than this blind loyalty, without reserve, without criticism of any kind, total confidence in one's own country, whether it be honourable or corrupt, equitable or unjust, perjured or faithful, 'my country, right or wrong!'

We owe some of the most beautiful expressions of the world's literature to this fanatical love. "The fatherland is the ground supporting us, the road directing us, the stream assuaging our thirst; it is a tree with its protective shade, a river to make our fields fruitful, a mountain to give us shelter; it is the church, with its peals of joy or a single bell tolling its sad message in our moments of despair."[43] This can be a universal picture. The Fatherland is the cherished panorama of England with its pretty stone villages, the cherished riverside of Brittany, the cherished lakes of Switzerland, and the cherished deep forests of Bavaria, the cherished plains of the Ukraine, the endless horizon of Siberia, the ancient college greens of Oxbridge, the skyscrapers of Manhattan, the cinemas of Broadway, the sandwich bars of the Bronx, the underground streets of Tokyo, the museums of Paris, the trattoria on the banks of the Tiber, the Sunday night traffic jams of Hamburg, the job centres of Barcelona, the prisoners of Buenos Aires, the psychiatric hospitals of Moscow.

The Fatherland is a holiday for the 18–30's, a trip to the Bahamas, a guided tour of Westminster Abbey, the gondolas of Venice, the Niagara Falls, pilgrimages to Katmandu. The fatherland is the air we breathe, the water we drink, the bread we eat, the sun we bask in, it is everything, and nothing, and what is left.

This idea has to be strong enough to "defy analysis", it must be "something obscure and mysterious"[44] to enable apparently sensible people to come to believe that nowhere other than on their little parcel of land can the ground be "as rich and fertile", that "nowhere can the sky be as gentle, the climate as temperate, the geographical situation as favourable", that only they have "the memory of a great historic past, the gift of a pure and eloquent language, the wealth of literature, of science, of art, the benefit of an economic situation full of resources, of an attractive society, of a humane and brotherly civilisation."[45]

An extraordinary phenomenon indeed, succeeding as it does in making man so shortsighted that for him only in *his* village or possibly *his* country do people possess the advantages and virtues to be found in them everywhere. This, arguably, could be enough to silence us, in total acceptance and adoration. But such an expedient will not do. Though we may respect the sacred qualities of the Fatherland, we must stop the mouths once and for all of rationalists, sceptics and detractors, by using their own weapons, that is to say, by means of a critical and in-depth study of the concept. To achieve this, we need a definition of the term. One which is itself the result of synthesising several previous definitions is put forward by the author Charpentier: The Fatherland, he argues, results from "a common ethnic inheritance, recognised geographical frontiers, original customs, distinctive laws and institutions, a language in common, a specific cultural heritage, a morally pure atmosphere and a unique way of life."

These criteria need to be examined one by one.

The nation is a homogeneous race. For instance, Yugoslavia, made up of Serbs, Croatians, Slovaks, Montenegroes, Bosnian Muslims, Macedonians, Albanians, Hungarians, Turks, Czechoslovaks, Rumanians, Bulgarians, Italians and Germans. Or take Brazil: few nations have so coherent a racial origin, as the country has only Portuguese, Indians, Negroes, half-castes, Italians, Germans, Spaniards, French, Japanese, Hungarians, Poles, Lebanese and Syrians. A majority of Latin American countries boast this kind of unity, such as Peru, where around ten different nationalities co-exist. And can anyone seriously maintain that the United States lacks cohesion, where only fifteen or so different origins are to be found? There are other examples, such as Malaysia, Laos, and in Europe, of course, Britain, France and Spain, with their dozens of widely varying origins, from their earliest history of inter-mingled races.

The nation is made up of recognised geographical frontiers, separating quite distinct countries. Go from the French Basque region to the Spanish, or from Savoy to Italy, and everything changes visibly, mountains take on a new look, valleys differ, houses vary, trees change colour, birds sing differently, streams sound foreign as they bubble along, even the colour of the sky is new. From northern France to Belgium is like entering a new world. You would have known you had left home without even having to cross a frontier. Temperatures, clouds and rain are different. Coal mines look different, workmen stop looking so obviously French. Inhabitants dress differently, laugh differently, suffer, weep, love and die differently.

The concept of Fatherland consists of a rationalised set of customs within one nation. Britain clearly has cohesive customs — take Scottish Hogmanays, Welsh Eisteddfods and English Morris dancing, for example. Such customs owe little or nothing to location and it is impossible to tell them apart. Britain enjoys truly national folklore.

The Fatherland consists of a network of laws, statutes and regulations which owe nothing to any neighbour's legal structure. Europe's nations have no judicial, institutional, educational, social or professional structures in common, and even lesser organisational structures such as road and rail networks, industry, finance and commerce bear no resemblance between nations.

The Fatherland consists of one common language. This implies that Switzerland, Belgium and Canada are not nations, nor is Russia with its 180 different languages, many of them official, nor India with its 782 dialects, nor Indonesia with 200, nor Burma, nor most of Africa's countries, where often the inhabitants cannot understand each other from one region to another, not even from one village to the next.

The Fatherland consists of a unified culture drawn from an artistic, literary and musical legacy handed down from generation to generation. In Britain this means such figures as Shakespeare, Milton, Purcell and Turner, but the British cannot accept the influence of such second-rate talent from overseas as Mozart, Beethoven, Racine, Goethe, Dante, Rembrandt, da Vinci and Michelangelo.

Finally, *the Fatherland consists of a particular moral atmosphere, an indefinable ambience created by our thoughts, our shared memories, our history (always glorious) which allows all men of one nation to flourish, whatever their origin, their profession, their culture, their class, their standard of living.* The Fatherland is a miracle which enables an American pianist to have more in common with a New York docker or a Chicago roadsweeper than with an English or Viennese pianist; and similarly a City banker can feel more at home with a Sheffield miner than with a merchant banker from Rome or Madrid.

Chapter 6
To Arms!

Every nation seeks security for itself. There are no exceptions, and politicians all over the world speak of 'national sovereignty' as the finest goal and primary safeguard.

Is this ambition justified? Some say not. They argue that such a constant desire for greater security reveals a basic immaturity, like a frightened child always hiding behind its mother's skirts. The strong, after all, need protection from no-one. In any case, this idea of security does not even exist in nature, where animals are forever on the alert, looking out for enemies who at any moment might leap on them and tear them to pieces. Existence, for them, means constant anguish. Why should we fare better?

The great majority of men, however, including most politicians and military leaders, argue that nations and the people who make them up, have a legitimate right to their security. The reason: since we have given our citizens the right to expect protection for the society they live in, the same must apply to the nation as a whole. This is a worthwhile ambition.

We come now to the question of how to ensure the security of the state, and there appear to be two ways to do so.

The first is the system of buffer zones. Any nation which has taken the major decision to maintain its security at all costs must begin by demanding a buffer-zone separating it from a likely aggressor. That much acquired, is that nation satisfied? Not entirely. Certainly the buffer-state is useful, but it is vulnerable. It would be wise to isolate it from its neighbour with a corridor. That too is obtained, or perhaps conquered by a feat of arms. Does that satisfy? Up to a point. At least it would do if that corridor were to be protected in turn, and so on until the end of the earth. Conquest after conquest has been born from anxiety, and even then, real security has escaped the grasp of our unfortunate nation, which failed to realise it is a myth.

Furthermore, this solution has all kinds of drawbacks: conquered lands, ever larger, become more and more difficult

to defend, their lines of communication stretching until they
snap, and worst of all, neighbouring states start to view
unfavourably such a series of colonies, particularly if any of it
has been to their detriment. They feel uneasy. Their own
security feels threatened more every day. As Kissinger said:
"The desire of one power for absolute security means absolute
insecurity for all the others." This is not ideal. Senator John
Sherman Cooper said in a speech to the US Senate in 1969:
"The pursuit of security through nuclear power alone will never
end. It will waste the fruits of the earth and make the labour of
men empty. It will increase the sense of futility, particularly
among the young. For we and the Soviets, with all our
technology, can be reduced to dust at any moment . . . This is
our present security."

The second solution is more realistic: every nation must arm
itself to the teeth, either by manufacturing its own weapons, or
by buying them abroad. Choice is plentiful, and dealers will
beat a path to your door; all you need is the foreign currency. If,
sadly, you have none, if your economy is a disaster, your
finances badly budgeted and your coffers empty, then there is
another way which succeeds nine times out of ten. This consists in
blackmail, using your strategic position as a weapon, with a
threat to change sides and sell yourself to the other super-
power.

With its new-found strength, your state will be respected.

In international conferences, in diplomatic negotiations, it
leads from the front, which is the best way to avoid conflict.
Chamberlain's "peace in our time" was an example of this. The
date was 1939.

Weakness, on the other hand, is a danger, allowing others to
become greedy. It is provocative. A healthy, well-fed nation,
with plenty of money, its banks prosperous and respectable, its
fields and roads well cared for, such a nation is a sacrificial lamb
— innocent, tempting, offered up to the famished wolf; it will
not last long.

To be strong is not enough for a nation. It must be *the strongest*.
It follows that its neighbour must become the weaker of the two.
Such a development is humiliating, as it would be if some tough
guy came along and kicked sand in your face. Determined to
put a stop to this, the weaker one enters the arms race in order to
catch up, and then outstrip the rival, who in turn feels threatened
again, and the vicious circle is established.

Total security may be an illusion, but that does not prevent people from desiring it with all their hearts. Absurd though this attitude may be, it is nonetheless praiseworthy. It is often linked with the idea that once security is achieved, everyone will disarm; which, it must be admitted, is quite illogical, since security can only be obtained by a constant updating of a country's armaments. Military and civilian leaders do not mind the odd contradiction in terms. The cry is: security first, disarmament second. History supports this attitude. Disarmament is today's great joke, the April Fool of foreign policy everywhere — about as realistic as the idea of a permanent peace. As is often the case with clowns, though, whose funny faces tend to hide a real sadness, the pathetic list of conferences on disarmament is a melancholic document which casts a pall over us all.

*   *   *

Was it to salve consciences? The Church was one of the first institutions to fall into the trap of a noble enterprise which the facts do not support. Signal were the failures. Converts were forbidden to take up arms again after their baptism, knights were asked not to make war upon receiving their spurs, and 'God's truce' was a plan whereby half of each week including Sundays and holy days would be free from battle.

In England, the new commonwealth of Cromwell tried to disband its army; in France, the pacifist movement did the same during the Revolution. Inevitably, the enemy at the gates soon changes all that. Britain, Russia and their allies thought about reducing their forces once Napoleon had been defeated in 1815. They thought about it, but did nothing.

In 1887, the Institute of International Law sent a document to the world's governments proposing a reduction in arms spending and manpower. Three countries responded: Uruguay reduced theirs by 25%, Argentina and Chile cancelled orders for two warships and sold off two others.

Disarmament became an essential subject for international summits in 1920, with the creation of the first permanent commission by the League of Nations. Conferences followed thick and fast, with little progress: 1922, a special congress. 1930, a conference on disarmament. 1932, another congress on disarmament, in Geneva.

The short interval between 1939 and 1945, one might have thought, would have cooled the ardour of professionals on disarmament, soothed by the rain of bombs and shells. Not in the least! In France, in England, only weeks before the blitzkrieg is unleashed on Europe, politicians talk of peace, and forthcoming disarmament.

In January 1941, President Roosevelt can discern ahead ". . . freedom from fear, which, translated into world terms means a world-wide reduction of armaments to such a point and in such a thorough fashion that no nation will be in a position to commit an act of physical aggression, against any neighbour — anywhere in the world." In the same year he reaches agreement with Churchill and Stalin to include in the UN Charter a clause supporting the lifting of the "crushing burden of armament", and urging nations to devote only the merest fraction of their resources to it.

1946: the Second World War has ended, but the Bomb has been dropped. The General Assembly of the United Nations resolves to set up an Atomic Commission, charged with the task of eliminating nuclear arms and all weapons of mass destruction, and of organising effective arms control. After forty years of intense discussion, the problem is unresolved.

February 1947: a Commission is set up to deal with conventional weapons. 11 January 1952: a permanent Commission on disarmament is born. 10 May 1955: the Soviets propose overall reductions in all armed forces and a ban on atomic bombs. No further development. 21 July 1955: President Eisenhower makes a dramatic proposal at the Geneva summit — an exchange of information on all military bases, and mutual agreement on carrying out aerial photography on all territories. The French President welcomes the proposal with considerable emotion and declares that from this historic moment the future of disarmament has changed. No further development. November 1958: All member-states of the UN become members of the Commission on disarmament. Why should only the chosen few have the right to have a good laugh?

7 September 1959: Ten countries from NATO and the Warsaw Pact meet in Geneva, seeking a closer rapport. The latest plan on collective disarmament is presented to the gathering. 20 September 1961: Moscow and Washington publish a joint declaration on principles of disarmament. 20 December 1961:

the United Nations approve this declaration and the setting-up of a new Committee, subsequently named Conference Committee on Disarmament. 21 November 1962: the UN's General Assembly passes a resolution in favour of total disarmament. 29 November 1965: the General Assembly requests a world conference on disarmament for all nations to participate. 14 January 1967 and 12 July 1968: Latin America is declared a nuclear-free zone and a treaty is agreed on non-proliferation of nuclear arms.

It is worth noting that the super-powers agree together easily enough when it comes to drawing up joint political strategies for developing countries. This is not so when they negotiate over their own weaponry, such as SALT, the strategic arms limitation talks. These talks began in Helsinki on 18 November 1969, after two years and five months of preliminary discussions. 127 sessions took place over 28 months. The first treaty (SALT 1) was signed by Messrs Nixon and Brezhnev on 26 May 1972, to last 5 years. As the treaty set a limit on the number of rockets only, and not the number of warheads or their power, it did nothing to stop the arms race, which gave the green light to an entirely new set of talks (SALT 2) which started right away.

Negotiations over strategic arms were not a hindrance to more general proposals being made on disarmament. In 1971, the Soviet Union, at the General Assembly of the U.N., returned to the idea of a world conference on disarmament. In 1972, a proposal was agreed to set up a commission, responsible for gathering views from national governments on the chances of organising such a conference. On 31 January 1973, talks open in Vienna on mutual, balanced reductions of troops in Europe. In July of the same year another conference — in Helsinki — on security and co-operation in Europe. In less than two years, it results in an agreement well beyond anyone's hopes: the participants agree to the monitoring of military manoeuvres by both sides. Subsequently as we know, those who attempt to monitor the Helsinki Agreement in the Soviet Union are imprisoned.

August 1976: in Geneva, the USSR presents a draft proposal banning all new weapons with a massive destructive potential. No further development. August 1977: after three years of fruitless negotiations, SALT 2 reaches an impasse, and after four years of equally fruitless discussions, mutual and balanced reductions remain frozen. Speaking at the October Revolution celebrations, Mr. Brezhnev proposes "a simultaneous end to the production of nuclear arms by all nations," and a gradual reduction of stockpiles "until nothing is left whatsoever". No further agreement.

25 January 1978: a special session of the United Nations is to be held in May, and preparations begin. France, which has turned up its nose at such feeble comings and goings, decides to join in the talks with some style. She presents a number of more or less original proposals, but with the proviso that her political objective "cannot be the utopia of a totally disarmed world". Unfortunately, this realistic point of view is contradicted by a passage in the accompanying note submitted to the committee preparing the conference, where the point is made that "the ideal of general and total disarmament has to remain the ultimate goal." There must be one version for internal consumption, aimed at military leadership and the staunch French public, and another for external use, for the 'charlies' of the diplomatic circles and for world opinion.

8 January 1978: 129 speeches later, the debate on disarmament at the United Nations comes to an end. Many admirably good intentions are expressed — to stop producing nuclear arms, to reduce stockpiles until they disappear, to stop increasing armed forces, to reduce military spending; but two quite new practical suggestions are put forward: to create a Committee on Disarmament, which will replace the Conference Committee on Disarmament in existence since 1962, and secondly to create a Commission on Disarmament, which will replace the late Permanent Commission on Disarmament. Summits on disarmament continue with new initiatives by successive world leaders — Mr. Gorbachov again proposing a total nuclear ban, Mr. Reagan talking of great progress being made. No further developments.

Were it not generally accepted that the people in charge of world affairs do possess all their faculties, one would begin to wonder. Perhaps the answer is that to them, these summit meetings are simply worldly gatherings where the company is good. How else can one explain this zeal for achieving a task which has *always* failed, whatever the way in which it has been approached?

Everything has been tried, except, needless to say, unilateral disarmament. Dr. Soper wrote in the old *News Chronicle*: "Defenceless good-will is the one policy that has never been tried . . . The moral effect would be to . . . electrify the peace-loving multitudes of the world . . . Through every government a new wind would blow and new policies would become practicable. Some other country would quickly follow the example and the whole international situation would be transformed."

Progressive, multi-lateral, controlled disarmament is more favourably viewed in political circles, but it has no future. There will never be agreement on any kind of international inspectorate, were it technically feasible, for the excellent reason that it constitutes an intolerable affront to national sovereignty. Not to be missed is the deep-seated irony of a treaty which calls for absolute trust to sign it, but to implement it, a system of control which implies mistrust.

Disarmament by categories of weapons has no greater chance of taking place. This system, which is presently under discussion, has got no further than any other. Within it is the seed of its own failure. Let us suppose that agreement were reached to ban such and such a weapon category, how can one ban in advance weapons not yet invented? How can the likely developments of present and future scientific work be guessed at? Should we prevent scientists from doing research?

There is also the old but popular trick of revolutionary proposals which have absolutely no likelihood of being accepted by the other side. President Reagan and Mr. Gorbachov are experts at these and have been making good use of them.

Add to that the recent developments concerning America and Libya, which demonstrate how difficult it is for the super-powers to contain and effectively block terrorism, waged as it is on a personal basis, even with state support. The use of super-power technology and advanced armaments appears to be too much of a sledgehammer to crack a nut, and more damaging politically to the nation wielding its awesome might than to the victim on the receiving end.

*   *   *

A nation which is strongly armed does not guarantee merely its own safety, but peace throughout the world. It would not be for us to put forward such surprising theories, were it not for the support of people of considerable worth, whose judgement is guaranteed by their culture, their wisdom and their experience. One should add though that other notables, whose culture, knowledge and intelligence are no less outstanding, think that anyone who believes that a frantic arms race is a guarantee of world peace, is living in a fool's paradise. This seems more reasonable. A wheelbarrow is made for carrying things, a car for driving, a boat for sailing, and in the same way, an army is made for fighting and weapons for killing. If on the other hand the army is good for nothing more than trooping the colour, cleaning up oil slicks or replacing striking dustmen, then its cost is out of all proportion to its function.

Since the cost of running an army is so high, then best ensure a nation making such heavy sacrifices earns the benefit of dominating its neighbours, since (as we have seen) this is the only way to ensure its safety. But to be logical: how does a national leader know he is the strongest unless he is able to make a fair comparison? To do so, he must observe his neighbours closely — what weapons and other military assets they possess. Naturally, they will do the same, which brings about a state of mutual mistrust. Should another country start to behave a little too aggressively, then beware — thoughts of conquests may have entered their minds. Vigilance is called for, nor should they be trusted. Should another nation appear to be rather more conciliatory, ready to compromise, then the answer is obvious — they are simply trying to dull our senses with their declarations of love. Under a smokescreen of goodwill, they will consolidate their position. We must be careful, trust no-one! Nothing they say or do is what it seems, beware false words, treacherous behaviour, turncoats, traitors. At the time of President Sadat of Egypt's historic visit to Jerusalem — a visit which took much courage and alienated other Arab states — after he'd spoken to the Israel parliament and people, it was necessary that beside the naively enthusiastic people there should be men like General Gur, who put things into sober perspective. He said: 'Let President Sadat be well aware that if he is preparing another of his tricks . . . we are not fooled.' Could anything be more friendly than that welcome?

Another country may fill us with confidence, it may seem to us brimming with good intentions and loyalty, yet how can we tell if it is going to last? Nothing is more fragile than power. A lost election, a referendum miscalculated, a leader gone, a coup d'Etat, a press campaign, an economic crisis, a financial crash;

from one moment to the next everything can change, a poacher turns gamekeeper or a lamb becomes a wolf, agreements are betrayed, treaties torn up, "the enemy is at the gates."[46]

An efficient government should never be taken by surprise. Suspicion on every quarter must be the second fundamental ingredient of any foreign policy worthy of the name, second only to security, of which it is in any event the corollary. A statesman must on the one hand pay friendly visits to other nations, shake hands extended to him, embrace their leaders, consolidate for the twentieth time their two countries' traditional links, and all the while he must quietly make use of his spies to poke his nose into his friends' affairs, look through keyholes, listen at doors, search pockets and steam open letters, do everything to check in case the traitor should hide some wicked project from him. That is diplomacy. Never be trusting, expect the worst, assume others are out to do you down, never believe what they say, or do, since you would betray them quickly enough if circumstances necessitated it.

President Truman once came out with a telling phrase. "When confidence has been restored," he said, "disarmament should at last be possible." It seems impertinent of us to doubt the realism of this idea, and yet it is hard not to ask how one can restore trust between nations as long as they remain armed to the teeth and as long as both remain ignorant of the exact military capability of the other.

It would appear that like so many personalities making statements of this type, the American President failed to take account of one important point: that the main planks of his argument — trust and armament — are mutually incompatible. This means that their opposites, suspicion and disarmament, are two points in a circle which forever encloses international politics. No power in the world can oppose this vicious circle: suspicion brings about rearmament, rearmament itself brings about increased suspicion, which means more rearmament. This inexorable, irreversible process explains the phenomenon of the arms race and resulting international tension. It is child's play to tighten this tension if it eases at all.

There are many ways of doing so. One way, for instance, is to make a number of provocative statements, nor is it necessary to wait for a lengthy period of peace, which tends to dissipate any zeal for action. A French general declares only eight months after the last bullet has been fired in 1918, leaving the participants no time even to catch their breath: "It is a good thing that our lads should remember and be ready to fight for the same cause again if it should prove necessary." After the second world conflict, there is no delay either and the armistice celebrations are still echoing when the allies, who fought side by side, start to call each other such friendly names as thief and murderer. Already, they declare, they must recognise the new enemy, and each wonders whether it would not be sensible to be the first to attack. Defence ministers work out what **percentages of the enemy's population and industrial capability** would be left after a good strong round of nuclear missiles; an article in the press describes the way in which the next war will begin; a well-known magazine details the progress of the forthcoming conflict and its happy outcome; books and films take up the subject of the third world war. Military tacticians compare the opposing armies, assess their chances, count and recount the number of nuclear warheads and missiles, time to the second how long it would take the Warsaw Pact forces to penetrate into Western Europe, calculate the probability of a **blitzkrieg attack on Britain or France**, throw suspicion on Soviet cargo ships which look as if they might be hiding missiles on board, and everyone holds their breath when major military manoeuvres take place, from Nevada to the Ukraine, via British air bases.

These pessimistic assessments are rather like the fire and brimstone sermons preached by some vicars: they invariably end up with a call to open up your wallet. Defence budgets go up, and it does begin to look as if the whole 'doom and gloom' scenario has been mounted to that end. It is worth noting that the military lobby, unlike any other, is the only one to carry out its own research (classified information of course) about its 'competitors' — information which is then used to justify its demands. The whole thing is simplicity itself.

No need to emphasise that any use made of psychological pressure of this nature must be discreet and subtle. A head of state must blow hot and cold, to avoid at all cost appearing warlike. He must give out olive branches with one hand, calling for dialogue and detente. With the other, he should be signing an order for a nuclear submarine, new weapons, bomber aircraft. He may speak of disarmament in international conferences, but he must speak of increased armament in private conversations, confidential meetings and closed committees.

These mental acrobats are on all sides. To the right, to the left, in the middle, among the working classes, the ruling classes, Socialists and Tories, British, Americans or Russians, among conservatives, and among liberals. The recipe is always the same, and only the style of presentation changes. "We must at the same time build strength and work for peace", says US Secretary Acheson in 1951, and Bismarck: "To preserve peace, our army must be strong". Churchill declares in 1954: "We shall lose no opportunity of securing an easement of world tension, but at the same time we must persevere . . . in our policy of upholding, at the necessary level, our united military strength." In 1955, Atlee declares: "Until there is an agreement among all the nations to negotiate seriously on disarmament, Britain must build her defences as quickly as possible and to the maximum extent." Eisenhower and Churchill make a joint statement: "We believe that the cause of world peace would be advanced by general and drastic reduction . . . of world armaments . . . we shall . . . develop and maintain the military strength necessary." "The best guarantee of peace is military strength", emphasises President Carter. In other words, to summarise the above, there is but one objective: to disarm. But one method: to rearm.

This is a brilliant proposition. Its daring may be the reason why it has succeeded so well, with every single country implementing it; whether it be vast or tiny, desert or pasture, wealthy or starving, lashing out all around or fresh from a peace treaty with its neighbours, every nation on our planet has one obsession: to arm itself to the hilt. A casual glance at military budgets tells the story. World spending on preparations for war, at a fixed currency, increased by 15% between 1970 and 1977, and by 60% compared with 1960. The number of men in armed forces has risen from 16 to 23 million. Add to them paramilitary forces and you reach 36 million men who train in all weathers, in every conceivable language, to kill each other as efficiently as possible. This is a far greater number than say, the number of university lecturers, of nurses or of doctors, who in the same climates and languages, try to teach greater understanding, and to save their fellows from sickness and death.

Developing countries make the biggest sacrifices. They do not hesitate to allocate a considerable proportion of their resources to the maintenance, improvement and completion of

their panoply of weapons. The league table that follows shows
which have the greatest enthusiasm, those that have joyfully
devoted more than 7% of the GNP to military expenditure.

                              Figure in millions
                               of US dollars

Chile	9.8
Egypt	8.7
Guyana	11
Iran	7.7
Iraq	10.4
Israel	16.9
Jordan	9.1
Korea, North	9.8
Kuwait	9.1
Libya	9.5
Malaysia	8.1
Morocco	7.3
Nicaragua	9.8
Oman	25.7
Peru	8.6
Saudi Arabia	16.3
Syria	14.4
Taiwan	7.5
Yemen, Arab Republic	16.4
Yemen, People's Dem. Rep.	17.3

(Details from SIPRI Yearbook 1985)

Comparing defence and health budgets, it is evident that many
countries prefer a barracks to a hospital, and a military
operation to a surgical one. This is especially so with nations
which have recently gained their independence, whose first
thought was, naturally, to build up their armed forces. The list
which follows consists of 32 countries where the amount of
money spent by the armed forces is between 4 and 51 times as
much as the money spent on health. This shows that the
governments in question are happy with the health records of
their citizens, with the amount of diagnosis, with the number
and facilities of hospitals, and the level of medical research.

There can be no doubt that they would not otherwise sacrifice
such fundamental social and human needs to the childish
pleasure derived from playing with tanks and rockets.

Country	Defence budget	Health budget	Comparison
Chad	22	3	7 times
China	28000	6000	4½ times
Egypt	1858	280	6½ times
Ethiopia	447	57	8 times
Indonesia	2337	428	5½ times
Iraq	2709	293	9 times
Israel	6599	590	11 times
Jordan	449	83	5½ times
Korea, North	1300	50	26 times
Korea, South	3603	129	28 times
Lebanon	267	34	8 times
Mongolia	180	20	9 times
Morocco	1120	211	5 times
Nigeria	2288	550	4 times
Oman	1187	81	14 times
Pakistan	1271	61	20 times
Paraguay	69	17	4 times
Saudi Arabia	17540	970	18 times
Somalia	105	14	7½ times
South Africa	2320	291	8 times
Sudan	200	26	7½ times
Syria	2255	44	51 times
Thailand	1240	249	5 times
Turkey	2523	545	4½ times
United Arab Emirates	1708	285	6 times
USSR	130000	30000	4 times
Vietnam	900	69	13 times
Yemen Arab Republic	386	39	10 times
Yemen, People's Democ. Rep.	124	8	15½ times
Zaire	200	35	5½ times
Zambia	516	87	6 times
Zimbabwe	478	103	4½ times

(World Military and Social Expenditures, 1983)

It should be noted that most European nations, apart from Greece and Portugal, have health budgets which are higher than defence spending (France: 40,000 to 26,446; West Germany 54,400 to 26,738; Italy 23,500 to 9,598). But the United Kingdom has a slightly lower health budget: 24,800 to 26,776.

Priorities are not in question. According to *World Military and Social Expenditures*: "No other social objective, no other official responsibility receives as much financial assistance as the military function." While the manufacture of arms uses up

more than 6% of the GNP of industrialised nations, only 0.3%
goes to the aid of the Third World. Nor does it go there in any
haphazard manner. There is no question of helping those in
greatest need, those in distress. Charity begins at home. It is
logical to help first those states which belong to areas of tension,
particularly where there is a military alliance with the donor.
Meanwhile the gap between rich and poor gets wider.

Taken on a world level, the average family pays more in taxes
to support the arms race than it does to educate its children.
This tremendous international competition never stops. Our
world is stuffed full of silos, bristling with guns everywhere,
crammed with airplanes, sprouting radar dishes on all sides,
and on its seas are thousands of warships, aircraft carriers and
submarines equipped with nuclear missiles. The super-powers,
the USA and the USSR, owned some 4,000 nuclear warheads
each in 1969. Today, thanks to the agreements on strategic arms
limitation, they possess around 14,000 multiple warheads, or
enough to destroy each other ten times over, which might seem
a waste, but you cannot be too careful.

*   *   *

It is a common failing of our century to think that everything is
recent, but the arms race is as old as the hills, and the concept of
deterrence is hardly new either. Hardly had man learnt to
fashion a weapon from stone when his next-door neighbour
tied it to a stick to make a spear. In no time a handyman
invented the bow, which enabled him to kill with precision from
a distance. Immediately a few faint hearts protested that this was
a devilish weapon, that there was no defence against it and that
war had become impossible. The rest we know. The bow was
superseded by the crossbow, solemnly condemned by the
Lateran Council in 1139, but which went from strength to
strength. When firearms made their appearance, there was
consternation. The same wet blankets moaned about dishonour
and treachery. Yet rifles and cannons did their work well, and it
would not have been sensible to abandon them. When machine
guns started their first deadly sweeps, someone cried out "this
butchery is not the way to fight!" When the first bombs fell from
the first warplanes in 1914, one general so far forgot himself as
to complain that such action was not playing the game. He
should have been shot for lack of foresight. A few months later,

the German submarine U9 sank three British warships with the loss of 2,500 men. Scandal, they cried, this was not a military action but a cowardly act of murder! A few weeks later, allied submarines were scouring the seas and murdering German sailors in the same cowardly way. As for mustard gas, which horrified all right-thinking men, that was soon being used on every front. It was said that there was no more cruelty in suffocating your enemy with gas than in drowning him with a torpedo, though moralisers might not agree. It was said too that every new method of waging war was considered barbaric, but usually ended up being adopted.

Much the same happened with the atomic bomb. From the instant of its devastating appearance, spoilsports forecast that we were entering a new era unlike anything that had gone before. So terrifying was the Bomb it would never be used — war therefore had gone forever. No head of state would ever dream of being the first to press the button, went the argument, and we had reached the balance of terror.

World leaders of the time were traumatised, which explains their melodramatic reaction to the Bomb. It is understandable — their imaginations had been blasted at the same time as the Japanese people, and this was still fresh in their memories. It must be remembered that the bombs in Hiroshima and Nagasaki had devastated all forms of life within a half-mile radius, and 35% of the inhabitants had died within one mile, either at once or after hours or even days of unutterable suffering. They had been burnt most terribly, skinned alive, the flesh exposed on face and hands, the shape of their clothes etched onto their bodies by the heat; they wandered, naked, shocked, in their stricken cities, cut off from the rest of the world, beyond help. For more than three square miles the towns had been literally flattened, steel girders twisted like paper, ships sunk in the port, thousands of houses burnt to the ground.

There has been furious argument about the number of dead. The official American figure for Hiroshima is 70,000 dead, not counting the soldiers in the nearby barracks, or all those who have died since and those who are still dying today in Hiroshima hospitals from leukaemia, lung cancer, or cancer of the stomach or the breast, all diseases which are a sequel to nuclear sickness. In 1949 the mayor of Hiroshima published what is probably a more accurate estimate according to which 240,000 people had died. The bombing of Nagasaki claimed

80,000 lives and between 50 and 60,000 wounded, according to the Japanese authorities.

None of this should alarm us. The whole business was far from the catastrophe some would have us believe. The Japanese were certainly dismayed, at least initially, and who can blame them? Those who had not been overcome by the explosion were understandably overcome by the temptation to paint a blacker picture than the reality. They said ten years would have to go by before the town could be inhabited again, that nothing would grow there for fifty years, that the survivors would be sterile, that their children would be deformed.

What happened? In two years, the town was rebuilt. The port was busy again. The population caught up with its pre-war level, then outstripped it. Thanks to the Bomb, ancient wooden houses disappeared to make way for swanky blocks of flats. Winding streets vanished and great avenues took their place, turning Hiroshima into the most modern Japanese city. The survivors, far from being sterile, have had more children than elsewhere in the country, and their children are unusually beautiful. The doctor in charge of the American Commission of Enquiry studying the effects of radiation said subtly that we must accept a certain amount of disappointment: not a single monster among the offspring of Hiroshima and Nagasaki victims. Not a single newborn baby with two heads or three eyes. A shame, but one might as well accept the inevitable.

Great strides have certainly been made since 1945. Greatest of all have been the developments in nuclear power, with the hydrogen bomb and the neutron bomb, which make the atom bomb that destroyed Hiroshima look like a firework on Guy Fawkes' night.

Confronted with such technical wizardry, the dealers in apocalypses resume their bleatings, and moan about the end of civilisation as we know it. Another crisis, they claim, and the holocaust will be upon us, the end of the road, the end of human life, of all life on our planet. How come we have still not become hardened to the stream of half-baked vociferations of these Cassandras? Their message is hardly original. Philosophers back in the 18th century were already warning of the life and death importance of disarmament. And so many since — particularly following on the first world war — have foretold that just one more war, and the entire race would lapse into barbaric ways, never to rise again, heralding the end of the world. Since when there has been a second world war, and never before has our world been so well populated, so advanced, so wealthy and so successful. At least, that is true of a minority. So much then for the cries of warning from the lips of all those dear prophets.

No-one can say that the hydrogen bomb is a joke. One device carrying a 20 megaton warhead (they are available in sizes up to 50 megatons, apparently) represents fifteen times the power of all the bombs dropped on Germany between 1939 and 1945. Or a thousand times the power of Hiroshima. But rest assured, its effect is not as much as a thousand times as strong: the temperature of the gases formed after a few seconds does not go above seven million degrees centigrade. A brick wall about six inches thick would only collapse if it was within about ten miles of the epicentre. Thermal radiation does not start fires beyond some fifteen miles, and there will be no second degree burns beyond about twenty miles. Nor should we exaggerate the amount of irreparable damage done to all living organisms, plants, livestock and inhabitants, as well as to water reservoirs and layers of ozone.

The Bomb has another advantage of considerable merit, and that is its cost, which despite appearances is not prohibitive. As US General Taylor once wrote: "It is the most economic of weapons, since in any future war the cost to the victim in destruction will be three times higher than the cost of the bomb to the aggressor." To take as example the destruction of Greater London with its inhabitants. One, perhaps two, bombs carefully placed would do the trick, which makes the per capita cost laughable.

No question then, of giving up a weapon so efficient in power and money. It must be kept carefully in reserve. That is what the United States, the Soviet Union and their satellites are doing, with their arsenals brimful of nuclear weapons. It has to be admitted, though, that these contraptions do have one drawback, and that is their effect itself. As soon as the potentially warring powers acquired enough hardware to destroy each other several times over, the gamesmanship became redundant. No further progress was possible.

That kind of pause, a movement arrested half-way, stagnation if you like, indicates we are on the threshold of an abyss. Realising this, our military and political leaders returned to the fray and rearmament took off again, following rather a different path which we can now examine.

*   *   *

It must be clear that moral or humanitarian considerations could play no part at all in this evolution. The military did not take the fear of a general nuclear suicide into account in their calculations. In the forefront of any rethink of world strategy were technological developments.

The first doctrine to be adopted was the theory of massive and immediate reprisals. This was more or less the point of view of Foster Dulles and McNamara. It can be understood like this: as things stand, if you launch a nuclear attack with no warning, we cannot stop it. (Yet. Hence the Soviet fear of Star Wars — the Strategic Defense Initiative.) But the lack of precision of your missiles will mean you will fail to destroy all of ours at one go. We will have enough left over to launch a counter-attack, which you in turn will not be able to avoid. In other words, you will certainly suffer irreparable damage. Two-thirds of your industrial capability will be flattened, one-third of your population wiped out. If there is a winner, he will have nothing to gain from the loser, other than ruins. War, which is about acquiring your enemy's property, becomes meaningless. What point can there be in undertaking such a ridiculous enterprise — we leave it at that.

Two conditions are vital for this 'anti-city' or 'second strike' strategy to succeed:

1. The enemy's military targets — silos and bases — must be largely immune from attack.
2. There must be no means of defence against a nuclear strike.

With a question mark hanging over both points from 1962, the world's military strategy undergoes a fundamental change.

1. Between 1962 and 1972, scientists made a good deal of noise about their latest developments. First, they created a delightful little monster with several heads known as MIRV, the Multiple Independently-Targettable Re-entry Vehicle. It is designed to change direction over the enemy's territory, and drop its nuclear warheads one after the other in carefully chosen places hundreds of miles from each other. Better still, giant strides are

made in terms of accuracy. It was still possible for Minuteman I
to wander more than a mile off target after travelling thousands
of miles. By the time of Minuteman III, the margin of error had
been reduced to a mere hundred yards, when even a margin of
two hundred yards would be adequate for the certain
destruction of a silo. In no time at all the margin went down to
fifty yards with the Soviet SS20 and to thirty-odd yards with
Pershing II. As the degree of accuracy increased, so did the
power of destruction, which meant that no silo could resist
modern warheads, even if it was buried a thousand feet below
the earth's surface. Earth-based military targets were no longer
invincible. The result was that a strategy aimed at destroying
cities was replaced by one aimed at armies. Privileged targets of
nuclear weapons would no longer be terrified civilians and cities
with their buildings and factories, but enemy troops. This is a far
more chivalrous attitude. You no longer destroy a country *before*
its army, as previously. The army no longer counts for nothing.
A welcome return to normal.

There are two ways of achieving this: the first option is 'first
strike'. This consists in launching a surprise attack of such
devastating power that the enemy's entire nuclear capability is
put out of action. There is only one round, and in a few seconds
the war ends in a knock-out.

The second option is a 'gradual escalation'. First conventional
forces engage in battle: tanks, planes, guns, footsoldiers. As
soon as things start to look a little dodgy, you bring in a tactical
nuclear weapon or two, and add a few more as needed. This is
only made possible thanks to the miniaturisation and diversifica-
tion of these devices, which have been adapted to specific
purposes.

Should your adversary have the bad taste to use similar
weapons as well, then item by item you up the power until you
reach, albeit reluctantly, the big guns. It will always be possible
to justify your action by saying you were forced into it by the
increasing stakes, and that you can take no responsibility for the
consequences.

Such is the speed of developments in research that even the
fortieth birthday of Hiroshima could give us little pause for
thought. Research has run away with itself, totally beyond the
control of politicians or the military, and even the scientists who
started it off cannot slow it down. Now there is a new
technological development to complicate everything:

2. Ever since his earliest days of warfare and therefore of existence, man has always dreamt of a shield which would protect him from his enemy's weapons. His adversary has always found a way of making such shields useless. This is a very old story. Lover of tradition as he is, President Reagan has just added another page to this saga. Defence correspondents, with their customary lyricism, have dubbed this initiative "Star Wars".

This development was predictable from the first launch of a satellite by the Soviet Union, in 1957. There was no reason why space should not go the same way as earth, sea and air, and feel the dread hand of the military. Particularly with politicians swearing one and all they would never allow space to be militarised. It is a bad sign when such unity of purpose is expressed, when agreements are followed by treaties, and resolutions by regulations.

No fewer than eight treaties have already been made relating to space. Among them: 1963, no nuclear explosions in space; 1967, no deployment of nuclear weapons or other weapons of mass destruction; 1972, no implementation of anti-missile systems.

All these treaties should have been a warning to us. Could we have been so naive as to believe that millions of dollars and roubles were being spent purely because of a desire to leave the earth behind for a while, the pricey pleasure of space travel, the serious study of the ionosphere, and the doubtful pleasure of walking on the moon? Even when a terrible accident occurs, like the death of seven astronauts in the Challenger shuttle, President Reagan is quick to emphasise the flights must go on — "we must reach for the stars!"

The truth is that for twenty-five years, the super-powers have been preparing for war in space with complete hypocrisy, covering it up with words of friendship and goodwill designed to fool simple folk.

At the time of writing, more than 250 US and Soviet satellites orbit the world. Their role is vital: military surveillance, telecommunications and navigation. They enable troops in the field to communicate directly with base. They ensure twenty-four hour transmission of information and secret instructions which cross and recross in the ether. They guide missiles, ships and planes. So subtle are their powers of observation that they can evaluate the production level of a factory or discover the installation of new machinery by assessing noise emissions; they can tell you what make of car is on the road; they can give you a reading from a newspaper's headlines; they can 'see' by means of a sophisticated system of radar several inches into the ground or below a carpet of leaves. There is no doubt at all that satellites are the aristocracy of today's arsenals, and a world conflict today would inevitably begin in space.

It should come as no surprise, then, that the two super-powers should have everything ready, including fully independent military command centres for the space arena, with impressive budgets (the USA's is twice the size of NASA's), and that experiments in space should be continuing unabated. There is no shortage of bright ideas. There have been experiments involving laying mines in space, firing missiles into the stratosphere from planes, making use of high energy laser guns or atomic particle beams. We now have killer satellites which play a few practical jokes on enemy ones, such as blinding their cameras, painting over their portholes, causing mayhem to their computers with extravagant signals, and finally blowing them up in a suicide mission once they have obtained every last detail of their present purpose. There is serious talk of installing a grand strategic base (remote controlled from the earth) on the surface of the dear old moon, once merely the subject of poets' lyrics and lovers' thoughts. Just one stage further, and it becomes possible to imagine a thousand megaton thermo-nuclear weapon, in geo-stationary orbit above our heads, to remind us that we are mortal. The bomb of Damocles.

To bring us serenity and reassurance, a mighty and ambitious project is born at just the moment needed: a space shield! Its promoter is President Reagan himself, who promises us that it will "free the world from the threat of nuclear war . . . save millions of lives, and indeed humanity itself." No-one can grudge him such a pious hope. How wonderful that at last the leader of the world's most powerful nation should have recognised the horror of nuclear war, the reality of the inevitable holocaust it would provoke, the terror of the ensuing nuclear winter. Wonderful too that he should propose a purely defensive system, which means a highly moral one, to replace the dreadful anti-city strategy, the immorality of which had never shocked the American administration. Nor the Russians, as it happens, nor the majority of so-called civilised nations.

Not having acquired personal sanctity as yet, the President, in throwing out this superb challenge, no doubt hoped to achieve something more than guaranteed peace. Such as giving American industry a boost; such as challenging the Russian might, imposing on them a new balance of power, and exhausting them with a new technological race. This last is something of an illusion, remembering that the Russians have tightened their belts a number of times since 1945 so as to meet the challenge, and succeeded finally in catching up on their rivals in levels of military equipment.

Where does the question of Star Wars now stand? Certainly not resolved, as continuing arms limitation talks indicate.

First, there is the inordinate cost. 26 thousand million dollars in five years, just for the initial studies. Estimates concerning manufacture and deployment hover around 400 thousand million, not including extra equipment to cope with non-ballistic weapons (cruise missiles and bomber aircraft) which would require another 50 thousand million. Taking into account the likely inflation of costs, between now and 2010, SDI, the Strategic Defense Initiative, will amount in all to some 500 thousand million dollars. A pretty sum. Not to worry — the money will be found, even if third world aid has to be cut back. Suffer the little children of the developing countries to die of hunger — there are still too many of them.

Second, there are certain unknown quantities. Ways must be found of intercepting enemy missiles at every stage of their flight: from the launch, through intercontinental flight, to re-entry into the atmosphere.

The first stage, when the warhead is launched, is the most delicate one to interfere with, because it occurs in enemy territory, which is not cricket. Also because it is so short, no more than 200 to 300 seconds. There is also the problem of such a large number of rockets launched at once, some 1,000 to 2,000.

The second stage, during which the warheads make their own way in a merry fashion, loosed from their parent rockets, lasts some 20 minutes. This gives us a fighting chance, at least.

The final stage is even shorter than the first. By this time, the warheads are in a hurry, and only 100 seconds or so will elapse before they reach their ultimate destinations.

There is an impressive panoply of methods of interception: laser guns fired from satellites or from the ground using giant mirrors in space to reflect their beams; 'electric' cannons also placed on satellites, and making use of highly destructive beams of atomic particles; finally, ultra-fast missiles launched from an orbiting station, from a plane or from the ground.

Nevertheless, atomic particle guns are still experimental. Lasers can be deflected by atmospheric turbulence, or through suitable protective devices, or even by means of rotating the missile on its own axis. The enemy could also resort to the idea of launching hundreds of mock missiles to draw your fire before loosing the real ones. It has been established that no fewer than 320 space stations would be needed to intercept the entire Soviet arsenal of nuclear weapons, not to mention the 6,000 tonnes of rocket fuel which would involve 250 journeys for the space shuttle. Add to this that the enemy, not being totally stupid, would seek to destroy satellites and space stations by all means at his disposal as quickly as they were put up, and they are particularly vulnerable targets. This means special protective devices, and so on, and so on.

Conclusion: a 100% foolproof space shield is not yet a reality.

All the same, the Star Wars project is unlikely to come to a stop, even though it is not that popular with the American people or their allies. On the contrary, we are likely to see development of defensive systems for both major powers, with the Soviets doing their best to catch up as quickly as possible.

This means that the whole concept of deterrence loses any significance. With no good reason to keep it alive, it might as well be buried alongside so many other concepts. The balance of terror did not last long.

This development changes everything for Europe, and particularly for Britain and France. To date, these two nations have been able to threaten the heart of the Soviet Union by means of a hundred or so missiles. Such a threat will gradually lose all credibility, with the advent of a Soviet defensive system in the next few years. If our submarines can be located and their nuclear cargoes neutralised, we will have lost all capability.

Does this lead one to conclude that nuclear powers, big and small, are about to put their stocks back in their boxes, heralding the dawn of the post-nuclear age? Does it lead one to believe that SDI will succeed in slowing down and eventually halting the arms race, and that President Reagan's vision of "a future with room for hope" is in process of happening?

Certainly not. The funniest side of the whole thing is that everyone will keep nuclear weapons, just in case the shield should spring a leak. Better safe than sorry. Better still, the protagonists will be inclined to multiply and diversify their arsenals to saturate enemy defences. In other words, deployment of a defence system will bring in its wake a huge outcrop of new weapons and the race will double its speed.

We return to the old saying of the Romans: if you want peace, prepare for war. How much wisdom there is in those simple words! Consider: if you want an understanding between nations, prepare a war which will divide them. If you want concord, prepare the cannons. If you want harmony, prepare chaos. If you want white, prepare black. If you want a thing, prepare the opposite. It is so obvious, so logical. It is not by chance that this maxim has echoed down the centuries. It is after all one of the most brilliant manifestations of man's intellect.

Chapter 7
A Clean Sweep

When Adolph Hitler said at the Nuremburg rally: "If we possessed the Urals with their superb raw materials, Siberia with its vast forests, and the Ukraine with its extensive fields of wheat, then Germany under the guidance of national-socialism would be rich beyond its dreams", no-one can say he was not being frank. There is an unexpected freshness about his proposal, a naive quality.

Our ancestors saw warfare as an economic necessity. No sooner have you hung up your venison than someone next door steals it. Jealous eyes are cast over fertile land, lush harvests. Starving Bedouins from the desert invade wealthy Egypt. Greek merchants urge Alexander to go to war for base commercial reasons. The Argonauts only set out to find the Golden Fleece because Jason had his eye on a development of tin mines in the Crimea. Rome enjoyed a very comfortable income from all the tribes who had to pay their dues, as conquered nations. Not to mention the market in slaves, although there were so many after Lucullus had won his victories, that their value fell to a few drachmas, and they became cheaper than buying a chicken.

It has been alleged often enough that the Crusaders, who left behind them wives and children, thought a good deal less about spiritual matters than they did about the temporal wealth to be gained. So many European wars were about avoiding yet another tax on your own people by acquiring next door's wealth. The Treaty of Amiens was broken by England because war, according to one MP, seemed "less onerous" than peace, under terms which were "a death sentence"[47] for England. To understand the Spanish-American War, you must not consider the Spanish action of blowing up an American ship, but consider instead the sugar production of Cuba, which the United States found attractive. The Boer War was sparked off by the murder of a British citizen by a Boer policeman but the real object was a British desire to lift the burden of taxation on the mines they were exploiting. Conflicts which still today tear areas of Africa apart owe their existence, not to the desire for freedom of the population, but to the question of ownership of mines containing copper, diamonds, gold, cobalt, manganese, uranium, phosphate and iron-ore, as well as oil wells.

Does the above lead us to conclude that behind every war there are hidden economic factors which are the real and only causes? Many historians and sociologists have made this leap without hesitating. We should be more cautious. A number of facts do not fit the theory. Is it not the case that most wars are waged by rich countries on poor ones, such as the wars of colonialism? Did anyone, except for Germany herself, claim that she was Europe's poor cousin in 1939, lacking industry, army or weapons? The USA and the USSR, who have constantly harassed each other since 1945, occupy enormous territories, have no problems of space to live in, possess vast resources and every conceivable raw material necessary to their industries.

*   *   *

Whatever the truth about the influence or economic factors behind the outbreak of war, the consequences of such a conflict are many and very positive. We need to explore three avenues: the period of war itself, the period of reconstruction, and the period of peace, or preparing for the next war.

First, a word about the cost of war, with a few examples. From 1853 to 1868, a total of fifteen years, war cost Europe's budgets some £5 billion, which is around £1 million per day, not counting colonial expeditions and wars outside Europe. The Turkish-Russian conflict cost at the very least £500 million, the Crimean, £800 million. The Franco-Prussian war of 1870 cost France alone some £1,500 million. The great wars of the 19th century, leaving aside India and Napoleon's expenditure, have been estimated to amount to nearly £10 billion. The money spent in the First World War (£1,500 billion at 1949 values) all told, could have provided every single family in the United States, Canada, England, Ireland, France, Germany and Russia with a fully furnished house with five acres, as well as every town of more than 200,000 inhabitants in the entire world with a hospital, a university and a library. As for the Second World War, which spread so much further and employed considerably more sophisticated weapons, naturally that cost rather more: at 1949 values again, the total was around £4,000 billion. We will not bore you with details of how many free meals, motor cars, cameras or bars of soap could have been provided for that amount. Suffice to say, for the curious, that one fighter plane is worth 15,000 tons of wheat, a destroyer costs as much as a block of flats for 8,000 people, and a war plane with nuclear bombs on board is worth 30 schools or 2 fully equipped hospitals.

Reasonable though these costs are, it is just possible that they impinge on the economy — though only to a minor extent. Nations at war hardly increase their overall debt. For instance, at the end of the last world war, Great Britain owed a mere three and a half billion pounds. France owed only just over one billion pounds to Canada, England and the United States. In 1945, France took on a modest little overdraft of no more than a billion pounds to tide her over.

Of course, national debts then begin to increase somewhat, what with pensions for war wounded, widows, orphans, compensation for victims of blanket bombings, repairs to roads, to works of art, to bridges, and inevitably, an increase in the number of bureaucrats to administrate all this. None of this poses a serious problem. It only needs a minor adjustment to income tax, which is what happened in western Europe with increases averaging twice the rise in salaries in the fifteen years after the war.

War tends to decimate currencies; good news for insurance companies, the state, and the whole motley of public and private creditors. All the little investors who had placed their carefully garnered sovereigns in blue-chip bonds before the 1st World War collected the money in paper currency after it — at a depreciation of some 80%.

On the commercial side, war allows the disposal of old stock. Every white elephant, all sorts of normally useless goods, stale food, out-of-date clothes, unfashionable shoes, shoddy and broken down electrical goods, bicycles eaten up with rust, all become like gold dust. A godsend for enterprising marketeers who had seen it all coming and made sure they were well stocked with as much old rubbish as possible.

Naval warfare and coastal blockades slow down or paralyse foreign commerce. This brings about poverty, which in turn activates the enterprising spirit present in every nation. Poor people will get ersatz: chicory instead of coffee, whale meat for beef. Rich people obtain what they need on the black market. Marketeers do a roaring trade and stash their money away for a rainy day. This happens in every war, and there will always be someone sharp enough to make his fortune while the rest of us are blown to kingdom come. The latter have the belated honour of everyone's gratitude, at least. No general ever forgets to praise his troops who lay down their lives for the generations to come. No political leader misses the opportunity of reminding his audience of the glorious heroes who went before us so that our lives might be easier, happier and more free. And the audience look around them and see millions of homeless families, of unemployed, poor harvests, no coal for heating their houses, and from the bottom of their hearts they thank God and their leaders for the great benefit of the war.

Every war brings major changes in our customs and way of life. Various wars have brought us silk, perfumes, leather goods, condensed milk, corned beef and lately developments in genetic engineering. Moreover, rationing extended the habit of smoking to women, who hardly did before, as well as teaching farmers and labourers the joys of eating beef, when they had restricted themselves to poultry, and teaching everyone the further joys of drinking spirits rather than a good old-fashioned pint.

No doubt about it, commerce thrives in any conflict. Between 1939 and 1945, the USSR's imports and exports increased considerably, as did Canada's, to the tune of 300%, and the USA's rising from 5½ billion dollars to 18 billion.

Industry does well in war. Heads of industry and finance make do with local conflicts, which they follow anxiously, when they cannot manage to invoke a confrontation on a world scale. During the fifties one could read in the newspapers that "the commodity markets are watching the possibility of an outbreak of peace (in Korea) with anxious eyes."[48] This would have had a terrible effect on the money markets and it was with relief that observers learnt of the breakdown of negotiations, which brought about the biggest rise in the Wall Street Exchange in months. Men were falling, but the currency was rising.

No-one should ever forget that the development of world trade is due entirely to war. No nation can expect a decent commercial expansion if it chooses to follow an intelligent political road, or makes a rigorous study of the market, or creates top quality goods, or improves on its distributive systems, or provides its clients with a better information network, and so on.

War offers a country an inestimable benefit by cutting off its imports of food. This forces a nation to step up its own agricultural production. Without such a need, there would be no analysis of soil, no sewage developments, no increase in mechanization, and agriculture would have remained at a primitive stage, doubtless with wooden implements and stone tools used by cavemen.

It was only thanks to the Second World War that Britain decided to convert her agriculture from mainly pasture to cultivated land, that she developed artificial insemination, that she took care to improve on the quality of seed and trained her farmers to a higher level of technical knowledge. The result was that 1942's harvest was the best ever. The same progress took place in the USA, where growth reached 21%. Artificial fertilizers helped of course, but so did the millions of new machines which spread muck on fields like jam on a slice of bread. Ceylon, the tea kingdom, and Jamaica the land of rum, abandoned their traditional products and turned everything over to maize and rice. Canada increased her produce of oilseeds fivefold. In 1942–43, Australia produced more than a million tonnes of meat. New Zealanders defied the threat of high cholesterol by producing 175,000 tonnes of butter in 1944. There were more cereals in South Africa, more vegetables in the Mauritius Isles, more wool in Argentina, more cotton in Brasil, than ever before. Everywhere, the earth was being squeezed like a lemon.

The most startling fact to emerge in the industrial sector was the extraordinary increase in production. Whether protagonist or neutral country, everyone concentrated on this phenomenon. No other inspiration — moral, religious or political — could extract such hard work, such inventiveness, such self-sacrifice.

Germany's war machine ran out of fuel: from nowhere, 32 factories emerged and produced 6 million tonnes of synthetic fuel each year. She lacked materials and labour: occupied nations responded to her polite enquiry and supplied what was needed cut-price or even for nothing. What is more, the exigencies of war forced her to put a stop to some waste which otherwise she would not have thought of ending. There were 20,000 types of electric lamps before the war: the number was reduced to 449 without visible difficulty, and 15 tonnes of copper wire saved. A particular weapons factory had 291 different machines: reduced to 8 it worked perfectly well.

The Soviet Union's industrial effort compared favourably with the United States. Two things made it easier for the Russians. First they did not have to establish a centralised system of state control — that had been done long ago. Second, the Soviets were lucky enough to have a large part of their country ravaged by war, which forced them to build new factories in the East and to exploit the coal, iron-ore and oil available in that part of the country. Siberia became industrial in no time, as did the Urals and Turkestan. Without the war, they would have remained an economic desert. Who would have wanted to lay cables and erect buildings in temperatures of −40°?

War is evidently necessary for good housekeeping. As we have seen, Britain, already suffering from a severe loss of agricultural imports, saw a dramatic decline in incoming materials, which naturally enough had been amply supplied by the outposts of the Empire. This forced her to become careful, wasting nothing. Coal dust was used for boilers; rotten cereals found a purpose in the manufacture of starch, wood shavings were converted to alcohol, old iron was made into steel, and even the nation's genteel young ladies used to five o'clock tea were put to good use in munitions factories.

Commonwealth and Empire found the same phenomenon, although to a lesser extent than Britain. Australians abandoned their pastime of importing rabbits and then killing them off once they'd become a pest, in order to manufacture machine tools at the rate of 6,000 a year as well as producing high quality steel. Rhodesia's copper mines hummed with activity day and night. Nigeria increased her tin production by 60%, and the Gold Coast upped her production of manganese by 43%.

In India, people who had spent their time in the lotus position, or sitting on a bed of nails or shinning up ropes attached to the clouds, suddenly found they had something better to do. Events forced them to learn how to build factories for chemical products and stainless steel. They succeeded, and a procession of armoured cars, guns, ammunition, parachutes and camouflage netting ensued, to the amazement of the sacred cows.

In 1939, Canada produced no military equipment or weaponry, not one solitary banger. Since when, she has become one of the most important manufacturers of military materials in the world; a long way from pioneers, hunters and farmers.

A Clean Sweep 101

South America received the special gifts of war too. No-one took such a place seriously, with their carnivals, their sombreros, their peasants and their theatrical coups. Who would have thought they could hide such resources as tungsten, zinc and other metals so useful to the manufacture of modern weaponry? No more poisoned arrows and scalping-knives, time instead for blast furnaces and steel mills. A lack of materials? Never mind, we can use local produce — in this case, coffee to make plastics.

The United States, for her part, required a colossal industrial output, on occasions actually able to produce no fewer than two tanks every hour in certain factories, in order to cope with equipping 11 million men, 75,000 planes in the skies, thousands of tanks, ships and submarines. Everywhere production reached an absolute paroxysm. Increases in coal, oil, electricity, rubber, synthetics, iron and steel, mechanical engineering and textile production beating all records. The levels reached were extraordinary. American military production was virtually nil in 1939, but by 1944 it had equalled the rest of the world put together. In every field, American power knew no bounds. More than half the world's energy, and nearly two thirds of all available industrial potential were theirs. America's economy was in fine shape.

* * *

It is a truism that war gives a real impetus to science and technology. Historians and philosophers have often said that weapons came before tools. The first machines were battering rams and catapults. The oldest profession in the world is not the traditional one of prostitute, but the smithy making weapons. The first roads were strategic paths, the first canals had a military purpose. Credit emerged from financing mercenaries, and surgery developed as a result of the military campaigns of the 19th century.

One could wonder why peacetime research is so badly off compared with military matters. The reason is simple: money is always found when it is a question of killing someone. There is simply no comparison between credit available to improve existing weapons and design new ones, and money for research into agriculture, medicine, architecture, education, health, comfort and culture. Money is always lacking for such minor doings, bureaucrats equivocate, contracts are delayed. Come a military discovery, and moneys are freed up, doors are opened, everything is made easy.

The Second World War pulled in a considerable technical harvest. Some elements stand out particularly.

With a fanfare of trumpets, we move to the top item: the bomb, herald of the nuclear symphony. Without consultation, we are plunged into dependency on a new form of energy which replaces oil production with uranium, solving anguish about penury only to replace it with new anxieties over radioactivity and accidents involving leaks and explosions.

War gave us rockets, rockets conquered space, enabling man to achieve weightlessness, to walk on the moon, to manu-facture and launch thousands of satellites so that future protagonists might photograph each other endlessly, and meteorologists might predict with previously unknown pre-cision the weather and tell us what may or may not happen to it tomorrow.

We owe the invention of radar to German bombing of London, man-made harbours to the Normandy landings, and the British idea of chemically treating the lakes of Scotland to increase the number and size of fish came about as a result of the death of off-shore fishing. Goodness only knows what that can have done to the Loch Ness monster.

No war, no nylon. So no stockings, tights, new-style tennis rackets, toothbrushes, and modern violin strings. No war, no prefabricated houses, frozen chickens, dehydrated vegetables, cooker fans, lightweight suitcases. Planes would still be made of wood and cooking would still be done in earthenware or iron pans.

The most noteworthy steps forward occurred in medicine. An endless number of discoveries including new methods of repairing damaged tissue, eye surgery, massive blood trans-fusions, new painkillers. It is fascinating to see how on the one hand man discovers new ways to rip bodies apart, blind, maim and disembowel his fellows with machine-gun and bomb, and on the other he comes up with new treatment to heal and cure. For instance, a new kind of orthopaedic surgery enables even the slightest muscular strength left in the stump of a limb to function, so that a man with no legs can learn to ride a bicycle, and a man with no arms can find a way of using a typewriter. Losing a leg or an arm in battle becomes almost a pleasure, and

one could be forgiven for practically envying such cripples for
their remarkable abilities.

*   *   *

It seems obvious that wholesale carnage invariably ensues from
the use of man-made weapons, since they are designed
specifically to slash, cut, gorge, burn, break, blow up or reduce
to mere heaps of bones the human body. The primary function
of war is to destroy, not just individuals, but possessions and
buildings too.

In Chapter 3 we saw how important this is for those in charge
and what impact such a policy can have on the enemy. It is now
time to assess the not insignificant economic importance of this
policy.

The first thing to note is that destruction is necessary for
creation. If I write, I mar and destroy ink, paper and pen.
Digestion involves an attack on and the eventual destruction of,
food by acid in the stomach. A growing foetus consumes a
considerable amount of its mother's energy. Plants can only
grow in soil broken down by bacteria, which must kill off a large
number of living organisms. In the same way, old buildings
must be destroyed and crushed by bombs so that new edifices
— bridges, factories and houses — can flourish. It would appear
criminally wasteful to destroy ancient houses or worn-out
factories in peacetime.

War, though, never seems wasteful, only inevitable and
therefore natural. So renovation of public or private buildings
can only take place through conflict, even if the operation
carries in its wake a few silly mistakes, perhaps some deaths, or
the odd shell falling accidentally on a cathedral or a stately
home. The end will always justify the means, whatever the
cost.

It is as if some magical element connected with battle enables
men to accept things in time of war which they would find
disgusting or completely idiotic in normal times. An enemy
soldier is seriously wounded by our artillery. He is lying there in
pain between the two front lines. Our stretcher-bearers risk
their lives to pick him up and bring him back to our trenches.
Surgeons rally round and operate, nurses fight to keep him
alive, and their efforts bring him back from the brink of death.
An hour before, we were trying to kill him. This is the way things

are: the left hand strikes, the right hand saves. Man destroys, man rebuilds. The more furiously he razes everything to the ground, the more frantically he can build anew. What pleasurable sights they must have been — Berlin, Hamburg, Warsaw, the Soviet Union with its marvellous statistics by the end of the war: 1,710 towns, 70,000 villages, more than six million buildings sacked or burnt, partly or wholly; 25 million homeless people; 31,850 industrial plants employing four million workers ruined, including 37 steel plants and 749 engineering works; 18 iron-ore mines producing more than 20 million tonnes a year and 1,135 coal mines yielding more than 100 million tonnes devastated; 3,000 oil wells put out of action. Also destroyed or badly damaged: 50,000 miles of railway lines, 4,100 stations, 36,000 post offices, 40,000 hospitals, 84,000 schools and 43,000 public libraries. Sterling work, to be proud of.

But then the same industrial strength which was used to smash cities and industrial centres with such gay abandon does a double-take and becomes a force for reconstruction. There is something very comforting about this, especially as the same directors, engineers and workmen, previously engaged in finding ways to destroy everything, are now busy sorting out how to put it all together again. Quickly too, as there is no time to be lost. Hardly has the armistice been announced than the businessman is announced too. He and his like arrive on their executive flights with their briefcases full of contracts, smart, efficient, bland.

Their role is to help the lucky loser, whose country has suffered the worst destruction, and to enable him to benefit from the latest technology, the best of everything after years of austerity. Industry must undergo a technological revolution. From 1945 on, the fearsome factories of war which had produced so many tanks, fighter planes, shells, guns, bazookas, and grenades, overnight become peaceable, producing motor cars, innocent tractors, sowing machines, radios, armchairs, saucepans and pencils.

*   *   *

Peace is merely an interlude between wars, and it is immediately time to prepare for the next one. A reasonable part of national production will have to be set aside for military purposes, and a number of discreetly-placed factories will continue to make weapons, as much for internal supply as for export.

Economists are agreed that spending on defence is of the utmost importance. Its effect is to stimulate civil industry through competition, and military chiefs do not hesitate to 'acquire' whatever they need from the civilian sector, thanks to their authority and influence, sorting out the best materials and the finest technicians for military use. The civilian sector is left with all the rejects. It is argued that armed services' budgets by their sheer size contribute to spiralling inflation, by increasing cash flows without increasing the available market for the public since their product is not for public consumption. The manufacture of high technology weapons does not even have a beneficial effect on employment, since it requires many fully automated machines and little manpower, apart from a few highly skilled workers. The American Bureau of Statistical Information on Employment has established that the construction of housing, schools and hospitals requires twice as many workmen than corresponding military contracts. Similarly, nuclear energy, the development of which is due entirely to the armed services, requires a good deal more money invested in it with a considerably smaller workforce than other forms of energy. As far as the environment is concerned, suffice to say that military requirements involve the use of a constantly increasing quantity of natural resources and non-re-usable forms of energy, and that the United States Defence Department alone uses up in one year enough fuel to run every bus in the entire country for twenty-two years.

The armaments industry is unlike any other. When it is a question of supplying weapons for home consumption, the ordinary laws of supply and demand do not operate, since the product is judged to be vital to national security. The state places orders with public and private companies alike. Since there is virtually no competition in this field, very little negotiation is needed over the price. Any order can be sealed with the formula: in the best interests of the state. Note too that a healthy arms policy can co-exist quite comfortably with capitalist or communist regimes, with authoritarian or liberal policies.

In the matter of exports, competition comes into its own. It can be fanatical indeed, ruthless in its methodology, including making use of calumnies, lies, blackmail, bribes passed skilfully under-the-table to generals, princes or influential politicians. In any event, the minute a new weapon is sold to one nation, its neighbours want one too. If they manage to obtain something more powerful, then the first country wants the same. There is never enough. Every nation can and does own a mass of weapons a hundred times more powerful than is needed. The only limit is in what the buyer can afford, although governments are more than willing to bleed their populations in order to acquire a handsome collection.

We have seen that arms are an unusual form of merchandise, not in the least adopting the usual criteria concerning value for money. For the manufacturer, they represent an almost inexhaustible source of profit, whatever their ultimate usage. Existing examples are of interest:

First case Arms supplied direct to the nation's armies or sold to third party countries are used during a war. They are destroyed in large numbers, and have to be replaced as they go along.

Industry is in top gear to meet orders from the state or from abroad. In either case, business is booming.

Second case The armaments disappear before they have been used. Orwell writes: "Even when weapons of war are not actually destroyed, their manufacture is still a convenient way of expanding labour power without producing anything that can be consumed. A Floating Fortress, for example, has locked up in it the labour that would build several hundreds of cargo-ships. Ultimately it is scrapped as obsolete, never having brought any material benefit to anybody, and with further enormous labour another Floating Fortress is built." Planes crash on first take-off, rockets explode on being launched, the German cruiser Tirpitz founders without firing a shot — a ship which used up enough electricity to light a town of 40,000 people, which cost as much to construct as a city housing 375,000 souls. In this case as in the one before, the result is the same, since despite its premature demise the weapon in question has to be replaced.

Third case The armaments are not used and remain in the arsenal. Never mind. In a few short months, they will be out of date and will have to go on the scrapheap. Sometimes, though, they may be thought suitable to be sold off to an under-developed nation, thus making a pleasant and unexpected profit on top for their owners.

Whatever the case, the manufacturer knows he will enjoy a constant stream of orders. This places the armaments industry in a unique category. It is an ideal merchandise. Hence the prosperity of those engaged in it. Today's exports to the developing nations are some four times greater than in 1960. By 1975 they had gone from 1,500 million dollars to 8,000 million. Three quarters of these weapons come from the USA and the USSR, but Britain does well too, fourth after the super-powers and France. The latter two countries do best if the calculation is made per capita.

As usual, every time our nation has taken a step towards greatness, back-handed remarks have been made and much moralising has ensued. Left-wingers, ecologists, and even some masochistic Christians have spoken up against any success story. There are a number of possible replies, which bear examination.

The sale of arms is not only morally justified, it is also of vital economical importance for the following reasons:

1. It would be criminal not to benefit from the present state of the world, favourable as it is to this need, in particular in the Middle-East which contains our greatest resource, oil. This is the only way to make an exchange to obtain what we must have.

2. The enormous turnover in export of weapons is vital to our weapons industry, which is itself of prime importance to our own survival. Before 1970, when the export of arms from France was worth well below 6,000 million francs compared with 18,000 million today, her war machine must have been in a parlous state even though it did not appear so.

3. The sale of arms is a blessing for employment. Millions of people make their living from it. The fact that millions more die from it makes no difference. Job creation is everything. If a factory creates enough work, it will be helped. Never mind what it manufactures.

4. If we refuse to sell arms to those that want them, rival nations will do it instead, leaving us with egg on our faces. Customers may suffer as a result, to the detriment of our own stocks. Good diplomacy requires flexibility, not rigidity. If we incline towards a high moral tone, we should choose a more favourable occasion when no material benefit is at stake.

5. Everyone believes that arms sold around the world are for defence only. Newspaper articles and official statements make this clear. When Britain decided to donate a thousand tonnes of military equipment to Zambia it was for defensive purposes, the Press reported. When the Soviet Union gave Syria substantial

military aid, that too was solely "for the purpose of reinforcing her defence capability". When the French government entered into negotiations with the People's Republic of China, then "as far as arms are concerned, emphasises our Defence Minister, these are purely defensive weapons." To sum up, when a weapon is bought and sold it undergoes a mysterious transformation: tanks, planes, guns and bombs only work in a defensive mode to prevent an invasion, stop an advance or repulse an attack.

What is more, public opinion actually swallows such nonsense hook, line and sinker.

6. Let us not forget that exporting arms is big business and the whole point is to notch up a sale. It can be achieved from the top via heads of state or their ministers on official visits. Or it can be done by the well-tried method of door-to-door selling, through exhibitions, or more specialised events. A very successful venture was Britain's ship the Tarbatness, in which every deck had rooms full of weapons for sale. Once a client came on board, VIPs from the services would fete him with banquets and booze. They even succeeded in selling weapons to states which had absolutely no need of them.

Another method is to double up civil and military options together. A deal might be struck for a new dam or the installation of electricity, but it would be dependent on buying a few arms too. Countries have been known to sell weapons to their worst enemies. Britain has always maintained an excellent commercial relationship with Argentina. This is not such a daft idea: it enables a government to point to the enemy's ever-increasing armaments to force public opinion into accepting a comparable increase in their own levels. This may not be morally very sound, but so what? Guns have no morals. In any case, everyone knows that in time of war many of our own soldiers will be killed by our own weapons in the hands of the enemy. Nothing new in that.

7. What would be immoral would be to prevent others from benefiting from the degree of security we have worked so hard to obtain for ourselves. On the contrary, our duty is to help them. Should we indeed pursue this argument all the way to nuclear power? Certainly. How could we be so mean as to refuse a developing country the same level of weaponry which we claim we must have? Would this not be a sign of a monstrous selfishness?

In fact, the proliferation of nuclear weapons is going well. If a sale proves awkward, then the nation concerned can be given the chance to produce its own weapon, through a system of licensing, co-production, staff training, supply of material piecemeal to be assembled on site, and so on. The multinationals have organised an ingenious system, thanks to their experts on law whose task it is to find ways around national laws without infringing them too much.

We have to face the facts. The smallest plant designed for civil nuclear engineering has the capability — by pulling a few strings — of delivering a number of perfectly acceptable bombs. This was proved in September 1977 when a so-called 'civilian' bomb was exploded in the Nevada desert. Canada's research installation at Trombay enabled the Indian government to explode a bomb on 18 May 1974. The Canadians had received a promise that the installation's production of plutonium would be declared and none of it would be used for military purposes. To which end, the Indians spoke of a "pacific bomb" which could not be construed as a real nuclear bomb.

The United States and the Soviet Union reached an agreement in 1968 by which they proposed a non-proliferation treaty. It is understandable that they were reluctant to see the rest of the world gradually accumulating stocks as big as theirs. It received a lukewarm reception, several countries refusing to sign, including France, Argentina, Brasil, Israel, India and Pakistan. Every single country, clearly, is determinedly opposed to nuclear proliferation, on two conditions: first, that they already have their own complete installations, civil and military; secondly, that this non-proliferation policy should in no way oppose their own legitimate interests, whether commercial or strategic.

A new agreement in London attempts to itemise a basis for international deals for civilian installations, and include a number of recommendations to be made by the vendor along the lines of those made by Canada, and which resulted in the production of a nuclear bomb in India. The agreement stipulates that measures may be taken against a nation violating the terms for purchasing a nuclear plant. Any question of imposing an automatic embargo on such nations was vetoed by France, guardian of independence and liberty.

It would be possible for the exporting nation to impose a clause allowing it to recoup the plutonium once it has served in order to treat it, but can anyone guarantee that not the slightest amount will be left behind to be used illegally? The point has been made that no country, having once mastered the technology to obtain plutonium, does not go ahead with acquiring it. If there are technical problems, then there is always uranium in its natural state, which most countries with a reasonably developed industrial base can enrich.

Recently there have been a number of technical developments which were thought to provide an answer to the problem of proliferation. One such was to prevent the enrichment of uranium, another meant plutonium would not be extractable in its pure form. But there is considerable doubt whether these proposals really work. Rather it is likely that production of military nuclear matter worldwide will continue to increase from the present level of some 7,000 kilogrammes each year, equivalent to 1,000 20 kiloton warheads (the strength of Hiroshima), and it is a safe bet that by 1990 a dozen or more countries will have joined the nuclear club.

Non-proliferation is just another myth.

* * *

The economic boom which almost always follows on from the ending of hostilities is very impressive. Factories go onto overtime, orders come rushing in, money is invested left, right and centre, fat profits result, industrialists are on top of the world.

This surge in demand means full employment, especially as a goodly number of poor souls seem slow to return from the war, and quite possibly will never be seen again. Workers' conditions and salaries have never been so good.

There is only one problem. It does not last. In no time at all the flood of tools, of gadgets, of cars, bicycles and motor-bikes saturates the market. They are no longer wanted, no longer of interest. Company directors anxiously watch the level of sales dropping. Order books are shut, everyone is talking about over-production. How can disaster be avoided?

The first way would be to increase consumption. And yet, you can hardly persuade people that they need not one but six cookers, vacuum cleaners, dishwashers, fridges and televisions. The consumer may be a hungry beast, but once he is full up he stops eating. A python, if he has just swallowed a sheep and gone to sleep, will stay that way.

We must turn to another solution. Since we have reached a surfeit within our own borders, why not export? Unfortunately, gone are the days when we could sell any old rubbish to the Third World and get in exchange their precious raw materials. From being for so long developing nations, some of them have now become developed. India, Thailand, Israel, Korea and Brasil make their own machinery, their own textiles and — worst of all — their own arms. With cheap labour, they do a better job than us. Another door closed.

Since we can neither increase consumption nor develop our exports, we have to think of a third solution: cut back on production. But this is a dangerous path to take. In its wake come falling investment, loss of capital, bankruptcy of smaller enterprises, redundancy in growing numbers. Unemployment is the result, and that breeds social unrest, strikes, riots, a split society. Long term, you are left with a recession, galloping inflation, a crisis of confidence with prices rocketing, the nation becoming impoverished.

To cut across this trend, to do away with unemployment, to release social tension, to give commerce and industry a new impetus, to bring back confidence in the Stock Exchange, to persuade investors to put money back into the system, every economist knows full well there is only one answer: a new world war. One (Belgian) newspaper pronounced in 1931: "Wars sufficiently well spaced out are the best cures for economic crises."[49]

World leaders are perfectly well aware of this truth.

Chapter 8
The Reaper

The outlook for the world is extraordinary. Every day our planet earth takes on board another 190,000 passengers. Every hour another 8,000 travellers join the ship, but how long can she remain afloat? In 1650, the world population stood at some 500 million. It took two hundred years for it to double to a thousand million by 1850. By 1930 it had doubled again, and doubled again to 4,000 million in 1978 — within thirty-eight years. In the pious hope that the narrowing down of time taken to double the population will not occur again — and there is no particular reason why not — there will be 8,000 million of us by 2015, and 16,000 million half-way through the twenty-first century. Even taking into account demographic projections, adjusted according to possible variations in fertility, the United Nations has estimated we will reach 13,500 million inhabitants by the year 2100 with average fertility, and 30,000 million by 2150 given a high rate of fertility. Rather a lot, in fact. Already, a good half of the world's population is underfed. It would not seem unreasonable to improve their lot, but that is hardly possible if the more urgent challenge is the continuing increase in the population.

There must be some solution. Contraceptives have failed to catch on in the fastest developing countries, as was proved by the collapse of the campaign in their favour in India and Bangladesh.

The logical move is to impede the proliferation of human beings after their birth rather than before their conception, in other words to increase mortality deliberately. Helping under-developed nations to achieve this would only be a way of righting a wrong we had committed, as we are responsible for their population explosion because of all the vaccinations, health care and preventive medicine we have lavished on them.

Nevertheless we cannot control — at least not yet — earthquakes, volcanic eruptions, floods or cyclones which occasionally ravage certain regions, and which can push target figures up to an impressive level. We should leave natural disasters to one side, happy just to invoke them in our prayers. A gradual cooling of the earth is more easily within our grasp, thanks to a huge increase in the number of planes clogging the atmosphere. They leave behind an accumulation of ice crystals which act as a barrier to a portion of the sun's heat. It might take a long time, though, for the new ice age to arrive, and time is not on our side.

It would be more realistic to organise a number of different catastrophes, which could easily be made to appear accidental, such as an explosion in a nuclear plant (the latest and so far most dangerous, at Chernobyl, is a good example), producing dangerous chemicals, or finding a way to engineer the collapse of a large part of a city. An American chemical company did recently wipe out a large section of the population of the Indian town of Bhopal. There must be a way too to disrupt railway signals and traffic lights to increase the number of accidents. Finding clever means of supplying drugs, alcohol and tobacco, and inciting people to debauchery in order to undermine their physical and moral well-being — these are methods well worth considering.

Mystery often surrounds the causes of great epidemics. Discreetly making it easier for them to spread would not be an identifiable crime or even an act morally to be deplored. On the other hand, it would be a rather more interesting solution than the preceding suggestions purely for its extent. Look at Spanish Flu which killed more than a million people after the First World War. A similar epidemic, given today's dense population and sophisticated systems of transport, might well spread relentlessly across the world. In no time there would be more victims than any manufacture of serum could hope to cope with. There is no reason why a general epidemic akin to the Black Death should not occur, when in the seven years between 1346 and 1353, 25 million died in Europe and 23 million perished in Asia. More modest, but still young, is the mysterious disease, Aids.

Such an outcome would be particularly beneficial in the Third World where the mass of people are suffering from malnutrition, and so more vulnerable to sickness. Herein lies the promising potential of a link between famine and epidemics, the former smoothing the way for the latter. Although several million do die of malnutrition at the moment (notably children), tens of millions more are merely weakened by the lack of essential foodstuffs — deficiencies in proteins, fats and vitamins — but do survive. A viral disease could sweep them away. The industrial West is also quite able to extend the scope of famine, by reducing the amount of cultivated land, cutting back on exports, switching from essential produce to more profitable goods with less or no nutritious value, or simply destroying food mountains if the price is not right.

Organised infanticide could give a considerable boost to the existing level of child deaths through natural causes. In the ancient world, in Arab countries resisting Islam, in some African civilisations, it was the custom to kill off new-born babies. Not so long ago in China, if the head of the family decided that a birth was ill-timed, either because it came on a day of bad augury, or simply because one more mouth to feed was one too many, he was judged to be entitled to do away with the child. Nowadays the Chinese only put girls to death at birth, reportedly. Sometimes the act of infanticide was less direct. For instance in Victorian England, the children of the poor were apprenticed at the earliest opportunity — aged five — to work in the cotton mills or up the chimneys, and from eight they went down the mines. They did not last long. In the Middle-East, in Africa, in the Far-East, the widespread custom of castrating children to produce eunuchs also produced more than a few corpses.

Another, rather attractive, project has encountered severe technical difficulties. The idea is to export large numbers of our overflowing humanity from this earth to distant planets and stars. The size and cost of necessary transport is overwhelming. Garrett Hardin, a professor at the University of California at Santa Barbara, has worked out that if all Americans took an 18% cut in their living standards, the money saved in a full year would only be enough to transport into space the demographic surplus of one single day. In any event, were we to overcome the costs, such is the increase in population that our entire solar system would become over-populated within two hundred years at most. The game is not worth the candle.

*   *   *

We come down to the fact that war is the only acceptable solution to our population explosion, both because it is so flexible in its usage and because it has support from all quarters, especially from people with high moral standards. The very people who react with horror to the massacre of new-born babies, or the exploitation of young children, accept with equanimity that such children, at the ripe old age of twenty, should be brought together and killed in large batches. This is all the more remarkable when you think how much more cost-effective it is to kill off a tot with no more expense than is necessary for nine months of pregnancy, than to care for, clothe and educate a child for 240 months to make a presentable corpse of him at the end of it.

That is how things are — war always enjoys a particular prestige of its own.

                               *   *   *

A really good blood-letting lightens the mind as well as thinning out the ranks. It is as though the body politic needs to purify its blood, sharpening its reactions and its senses. Hence the speedy response of society and the almost immediate resurgence in population growth. If the military and the Church exert a strong influence within a state, then that growth is accelerated.

Through all time, religion has trumpeted the virtue of reproduction. In Buddhism, a man is without honour if he has no progeny to pay off his debt to his ancestors. In Japan, Shintoism states that a lack of children is a sacrilege against religion and state. Catholics, concerned with increasing the troops pitted against the heretics, believe that man disobeys God's will and challenges the divine plan if he limits the size of his family.

Military leaders have an obvious axe to grind over the size of the population. First, because they have never been able to dispense with the old-fashioned concept of the 'big battallions'. To achieve those, they are greedy for young children and will nurture them until they reach the right age for the sacrifice. Secondly they know that the pressure of too big a population creates aggression, imperialism and violence. Pushing people over the edge and into war becomes child's play. That is why governments start with legislation in favour of greater pro-creation when war is in their minds. The French did just that under Louis XIV, as did the Germans and the Italians from 1933 with decrees favouring large families. Japan's government published a law in 1941 forcing men to marry by the age of 25, women by the age of 21, and couples had to come up with at least five children.

As soon as demographic pressure starts to build in the state cooker, leaders have their cue to declare that the nation must have more space or chaos will ensue, with all those mouths to feed. They naturally prefer to spread outwards before internal problems bring them down. Hence the Romans with their policy of expansion; the barbarians in turn taking on the might of the Empire in search of more fertile and less populated lands; Japan with her insular problems taking on the Russians with their space; fascist Italy devouring Ethiopia. There is no shortage of examples.

It is clear that there is a very special relationship between war and demography. The military machine starts the cycle off by encouraging a growth in population; with a surfeit of young people, the nation acquires an increasingly aggressive stance. War breaks out, and results in a more or less large hole in the population. As the most warlike people always have the greatest vitality and are the most fertile, losses are soon made up and the population grows again. The French under Henry IV could count on a more or less permanent engagement against the Turk; the English under Henry VIII and Elizabeth I enjoyed the same advantage of constant warfare against Spain, the Netherlands or even France. They could countenance peace in the knowledge that the pressure valve was available. Such is no longer the case. The growth of population world-wide has exceeded all hope of control unless we accept ever more devastating wars. Two new elements enter into consideration.

First, war has become total, with virtually the entire population involved. In the Hundred Years War, only a few thousand were involved in a population of 20 million. Even Napoleon only managed to involve a million out of 25 million. In 1914, the number grew to around 4 million in each country where populations were around 40 million or so. Now women are involved too, and of course civilians cannot help but be pulled in. Just as the earliest primitive tribes expected every tribesman to participate in any battle, so do we now.

Secondly, we have the production of ever more precise and devastating weapons. One optimist wrote in 1914 that the more accurate weapons are, the fewer people are killed or wounded, according to statistics. Presumably people needed to be reassured in 1914. The fact is that the number of people killed has invariably grown with the increasing sophistication of weaponry.

It is perfectly true that some early campaigns waged with straightforward non-technological arms did manage to account for a handsome number of souls. Caesar, it is thought, took care of 3 million — as many as Napoleon. Great minds think alike. The Tartars and Mongols are credited with 25 million corpses to their names. The Crusaders ran up quite a bill: somewhere between 2 and 6 million, Christians and Infidels mixed.

The Renaissance, though, seemed to value life. It is said that at the battle of Anghiari 20,000 soldiers fought it out for four long hours with the loss of only one man, and then only because he fell off his horse!

The Spanish War of Succession resulted in only 400,000 dead, Crimea 785,000; the American Civil War 800,000, the war in Paraguay 1 million. From the Treaty of Westphalia to 1856 a mere 8 million perished in battle. In the few years from 1853 to 1866 Europe lost only 1,743,000 men. The Franco-Prussian war sorted out some 600,000, with France's Second Empire as a whole accounting for 1,500,000. 15 million in all as a grand total for Europe in the 19th century.

The situation improves from the turn of the century. The First World War is reckoned to have cost some 8,700,000 at least, though some estimates rise to 11 or even 12 million, but statisticians maintain that one should add a similar number of indirect deaths, so around 25 million in all. The Second World War total is thought to be of the order of 38 million, but some historians think this figure is over-modest and they put it nearer 60 million or even 100 million. We should be wary of greedy over-estimates, and be satisfied with rounding the figures off at 10 million for the First War, and 50 for the Second. Leave it at that.

It is estimated that in the world as a whole, a figure of 40 million killed each century is not unreasonable. That means 2 thousand million in 5,000 years of civilisation, and 5 thousand million since man's adventure on earth began. If you buried the dead of the wars of just one century side by side, they would encompass the earth, and their blood would fill 3 million barrels.

Two points worth noting here: one, that the proportional percentage of civilians among those killed increases all the time.

In 1914–18, it stood at 13%. In 1939–45, it leapt to 70%, and in Korea to 84%. Secondly, that the losses curve leaves no doubt whatsoever about the nature of the next world conflict. It will be nuclear, because there would be no way of achieving the level of losses by means of conventional warfare (some 360 million dead are needed statistically).

The value we place on human life is put into its proper perspective by the enormous losses sustained in war, in particular in modern warfare. No longer can we grieve over the loss of one person or one family, with the modern-day necessity to reckon on millions of dead in one go. On the contrary, we need to accept with equanimity that whole sections of the population may be done away with in certain circumstances. Numerous heads of state have this attitude and as long as the cause is good they can quite calmly reckon on losing thousands if not millions of souls. To save the nation, you must be ready to sacrifice down to the very last man, woman or child. This is one way of resolving your problem, since the nation, being the sum total of the individuals, will have disappeared.

Now that hygiene and medicine have made such progress, the heaviest losses can be sustained without undue anxiety, as they will be made good virtually overnight. After the holocaust of 1939–45, most of the nations engaged in the battle brought the numbers of their population back to the starting-point within five years. We should not despair, though. The next war will enable us to achieve something more permanent, given that it will not be long in coming and our resolution will be firm. As one thinker wrote, great massacres are the hallmark of great times, and ours is a memorable epoch, surely.

*   *   *

Last, but not least, of the reasons why we are said to prefer war to every other means of putting a break on the world's population acceleration, is the fact that it is a perfect method of selection for humanity, apart from its intrinsic qualities, that is. The foremost authorities agree on this. For instance, here is a view expressed by General von Bernhardi: "Wherever you may look in nature, you will find that war is a fundamental law of evolution. Already accepted in previous centuries, this great truth was convincingly demonstrated in our time by Charles Darwin. He proved that nature is governed by the struggle for survival, and that this very struggle with its apparent ruthlessness produces a system of selection which eliminates the weak and feeble."

That is clear enough. Reference to Darwin himself must surely confirm in his works ideas promoted by von Bernhardi. A conscientious general would doubtless not use the thoughts of a philosopher without reading his books.

And so it is: Darwin's most important themes all tend in that direction; the animal kingdom's fine evolution, from the most humble creature all the way to man himself, has occurred through natural selection, itself the result of the struggle for life. The only slight difference between the philosopher and the general is that to the former it is by no means a question of a struggle involving the extermination of one species by another, or the survival of the fittest, but the survival of the group which is best suited to its environment, the one which is most adept at acquiring the necessities of life — food, air and water, light and shade, space to live and play. Otherwise, every fly, every ant would long since have disappeared from the earth. It has been argued that the real sense of 'struggle' is not war, but effort. Darwin writes: "I use this term (struggle for existence) in a large and metaphorical sense . . . a plant on the edge of the desert is said to struggle for life against the drought, though more properly it should be said to be dependent on the moisture." The author of *The Origin of the Species* goes on: "The bravest men, who were always willing to come to the front in war, and who freely risked their lives for others, would on an average perish in larger numbers than other men." Turning to the practice of conscription, Darwin makes his case worse: "The finest young men are taken by conscription or enlisted. They are thus exposed to early death during war . . . The shorter or feebler men, with poor constitutions, are left at home, and consequently have a much better chance of marrying and of propagating their kind." So Darwin does admit that a system of selection operates through war. It is simply rather different from the one propounded by von Bernhardi. Instead of destroying the weak, it massacres the strong.

This statement needs more careful examination. It is hard to deny that among primitive peoples the strongest and bravest men who throw themselves against the enemy with savage cries, are the ones most likely to return from battle with an arrow stuck in one eye or a nasty hole in the side from a passing spear. But the problem becomes more complex in modern times and a distinction must be made between soldiers and civilians.

Whether we are dealing with a professional army or, as is more often the case, with enlisted men, the armed forces of a country at war are made up of individuals who have already undergone a careful selection process. Not just anyone is chosen. The man-eating machine has delicate taste buds. It requires strong men of good aspect, healthy-looking and mentally as well as physically fit.

This flower of the nation, this elite will be kept apart from the rest of the population by the exigencies of war, thus effectively prevented from reproducing healthy children just when the country needs them most, being sent off instead to be mown down at the Front. What better selection could there be, than to see the best killed? Cowards and runts, on the other hand, wait for the battle to end, come out of their hiding places, kill off the wounded, rob the dead, and return home as heroes.

The brave spared by bullets, will often fall victim to disease more readily than civilians, as statistics prove. Weariness, long marches, lack of hygiene and sleep, rigours of climate, and nervous tension are the principal causes. Between the years 1870–1880, death through typhoid amounted to 5 per 1000 of the civilian population, but 30 per 1000 in the army. Here too, death took the best. It is often the case that disease does away with more soldiers than enemy guns can. In the American Civil War, of the 304,369 North American soldiers who died, 186,216 never achieved a glorious end on the field of battle. The same happened for Britain in the war against Napoleon or in the Crimea. Death through sickness took a greater toll than death in battle. It is said that Wellington's army had a sickness rate of about 20 in every 100 men, and that in October 1811, 330 in every 1000 were in hospital. As for the puritan armies of Cromwell, they are accused of bringing to Scotland both the Protector's authority and that military disease syphilis.

The lucky lads who manage to escape enemy bullets, typhus and dysentery, go home in a sorry state at the ending of hostilities. Some of them expire shortly afterwards. Others will try to overcome great difficulties so that they may return to a normal life and have children. There is no shortage of women. War decimates the male population, leaving an excess of frustrated females. But demobbed soldiers are battle-weary, depressed, perhaps suffering the effects of poison gas. They are hardly up to procreation. Even if they have avoided contact with defoliant poisons, there is a risk of creating stunted children.

Height is a particular problem with the children of ex-soldiers. After every war, recruiting authorities have found it necessary to lower the minimum requirement to make up the numbers. In the reign of Louis XIV in France, the minimum required height was 1.624 metres. Napoleon brought it down in 1799 to 1.598 m., then five years later to 1.544 m. — an army of dwarfs! True enough he was no giant himself. At the Restoration, it rose again to 1.57 m., then down again to 1.54 m., when the war with Spain occurred. Children born after the Franco-Prussian war of 1870 in both countries were said to be "of very mediocre quantity, of dreadful quality."[50] These entire generations of pocket-sized individuals have the effect of increasing the numbers rejected from the services. In 1827 it reached over 43% in France, and in 1900, more than half the recruits in England were rejected.

Thinking superficially, one might conclude that as far as civilians are concerned bombs do not choose where to fall, hitting the good and the bad equally, with no selection process at work. This is not so. Bombs do actually prefer those most exposed to them, those responsible for defence work such as firemen, stretcher-bearers, medics, nurses — in other words, those most prepared to devote themselves despite the danger — yet again.

This selection game goes badly wrong given our nuclear anti-city strategy. Selective criteria cannot cope with global destruction where every victim is equally privileged. Luckily though, as we have said before, this strategy is gradually making way for an anti-troop system giving back his rights to the professional fighter, particularly his first right to serve as a target for enemy weapons. At once war regains its vital demographic function traditionally-held: tearing to pieces, burning or destroying by radiation the most ardent, the most handsome, the most promising young people dedicated to the propagation of the country's finest talent, and tenderly preserving the disabled, the rickety, the epileptic, the debilitated and the cretinous for the propagation of their own kind.

Chapter 9
The Poetry of War

The greatest works of Antiquity were military chronicles: Xenophon's *Anabasius*, Caesar's *Gallic Wars*. Simonides' *Thermopylae* gives a brief flavour of the birth of the heroic poem:

> Go tell the Spartans, thou that passest by,
> That here, obedient to their laws, we lie.

The sacrifice of man for nation begins early. France's great hero of the 8th century, Roland, is commemorated in the powerful epic *The Song of Roland*, translated here by Dorothy L. Sayers:

> And Roland saith: "Fair Fellow Oliver,
> You were own son unto Duke Renier,
> That held the marches of the Vales of Runers,
> To shatter shield or break lance anywhere,
> And from their seat proud men to overbear,
> And cheer the brave with words of counsel fair,
> And bring the cruel to ruin and despair,
> No knight on earth was valiant as you were."

This influence of war on poetry, numbering as it does such works as the *Ramayana, The Iliad* and *The Aeneid*, pursues its way through history to culminate in the glorious outpourings of the First World War. There is none so guaranteed to bring a tear to every eye as Rupert Brooke's *The Soldier*:

> If I should die, think only this of me:
>   That there's some corner of a foreign field
> That is for ever England. There shall be
>   In that rich earth a richer dust concealed;
> A dust whom England bore, shaped, made aware,
>   Gave, once, her flowers to love, her ways to roam,
> A body of England's breathing English air,
>   Washed by the rivers, blest by suns of home.

This theme of sacrifice in a foreign field, for a greater cause, found its apotheosis in John McCrae's *In Flanders Fields*, repeated every year since 1918 at the annual Remembrance:

> In Flanders fields the poppies blow
> Between the crosses, row on row,
> That mark our place;

But the words addressed to future generations, urging us to continue the fight, come later:

> Take up our quarrel with the foe:
> To you from failing hands we throw
> The torch; be yours to hold it high.
> If ye break faith with us who die
> We shall not sleep, though poppies grow
> In Flanders fields.

The message to the fighting man was clear:

> The fighting man shall from the sun
> Take warmth, and life from the glowing earth;
> Speed with the light-foot winds to run,
> And with the trees to newer birth;
> And find, when fighting shall be done,
> Great rest, and fullness after dearth.

Julian Grenfell ends the above poem, *Into Battle* (1915) with the words:

> The thundering line of battle stands,
> And in the air Death moans and sings;
> But Day shall clasp him with strong hands,
> And Night shall fold him in soft wings.

Throughout history, there has been a persistent idea that death is a kind of reward for battle, the natural outcome, devoutly to be wished:

> What finer end than the death of a warrior
> Who falls on a sudden in the heat of the battle? . . .
> Without fear he meets death the enchanteress:
> Calmly he dies, without regret or sadness.
> . . . .
> The bodies to the sound of the trumpet we bury —
> And of the drum — for death makes men merry!
>
> (Martin de Condé.)

Merry certainly the survivors, for the death of their fellow soldiers is not only honourable, but paves the way for rapid promotion of those that are left. There is nothing like tangible reward to maintain morale, both in the army and in the nation as a whole.

To ensure enthusiasm and prevent soldiers from becoming too friendly towards their traditional enemies, the most pacific of men — the men of the cloth themselves — must keep the flag of hatred flying. Abbot Bellouard penned these words addressed to the French infantryman, translated here as the archetypal British Footslogger 'Tommy':

> Tommy likes to bite a German,
> And he doesn't mind the smell, and he doesn't mind the taste . . .

Who is this German to be bitten? He is nothing more than a beast:

> The Boche is a skunk or a pig or a rat . . .
> His eyes are protruding, all glaucous and fat.
> To be held by their look is certain death,
> Like creeping mustard gas racking your breath.
>
> (Jules Pech.)

What possible feelings can anyone have towards such a creature other than loathing?

> Offer with pride to the world our hate.
> Hate is a blessed word, say it in your thoughts,
> Hate is a blessed word, say it in your sleep,
> Hate is a blessed word, say it when you wake . . .
> Teach it to your children, teach them how to hate.
>
> (Jules de Marthold.)

A new element arrived between the world wars to replace blind patriotism — political awareness. Its finest examples indicate a new way of commending warfare that has a familiar old-fashioned ring:

> Our fight's not won till the workers of all the world
> Stand by our guard on Huesca's plain
> Swear that our dead fought not in vain,
> Raise the red flag triumphantly
> For Communism and for liberty.
>
> (John Cornford.)

I read of a thousand killed.
And am glad because the scrounging imperial paw
Was there so bitten.

(Bernard Spencer.)

Out of the ashes of despair of 1918 there arose a new hope,
built upon no expectation. Here is Herbert Read in *To a Conscript
of 1940*:

A soldier passed by me in the freshly fallen snow
His footsteps muffled, his face unearthly grey;
And my heart gave a sudden leap
As I gazed on a ghost of five-and-twenty years ago.

. . .you, my brother and my ghost, if you can go
Knowing that there is no reward, no certain use
In all your sacrifice, then honour is reprieved
To fight without hope is to fight with grace,
The self reconstructed, the false heart repaired.

All too soon, though, the essence of faith in battle and death
for a cause returns, as it always has, as it always must:

Underneath this wooden cross there lies
A Christian killed in battle. You who read,
Remember that this stranger died in pain;
And passing here, if you can lift your eyes
Upon a peace kept by a human creed,
Know that one soldier has not died in vain.

(Karl Shapiro.)

We would not want to give the impression that earlier times
paid less tribute to war. Turning to the 19th century and one of
the great lyrical writers whose name conjures up daffodils rather
than guns, we find this pastoral eulogy:

Vanguard of liberty, ye Men of Kent,
Now is the time to prove your hardiment!
To France be words of invitation sent!
They from their fields can see the countenance
Of your fierce war, may ken the glittering lance,
And hear you shouting forth your brave intent.

No parleying now! In Britain is one breath;
We are all with you now from shore to shore;
Ye Men of Kent, 'tis victory or death!

No less a personage than William Wordsworth. Meanwhile, across that Channel, we have French sentiments; addressed in this instance by a general to his sword:

> Slice the air with a sweeping blow,
> Pierce their hearts and burn them like fire!
> Bravely now! Make the rivers of blood flow,
> Strike at their helmets and the faces below —
> O my sword, instrument of divine ire!

And across another frontier, a similar German fervour:

> O Germany, now is the time for hate!
> Heart of steel, trample on the devil's race
> And let their corpses pile up to the very skies,
> Smoking flesh, smashed bones and staring eyes . . .
> . . . No prisoners, and for every enemy heart — a bayonet!

Every nation has its particular pride, and for Britain, it is the sea. Once on board ship, the natural British reserve is blown away and a surge of patriotism rises from the deep:

> Ye Mariners of England
> That guard our native seas!
> Whose flag has braved a thousand years
> The battle and the breeze!
>
> The spirits of your fathers
> Shall start from every wave —
> For the deck it was their field of fame,
> And ocean was their grave:
> Where Blake and mighty Nelson fell
> Your manly hearts shall glow,
> As ye sweep through the deep,
> While the stormy winds do blow!
> While the battle rages loud and long
> And the stormy winds do blow.
>
> (Thomas Campbell.)

Stirring stuff. But for sheer pathos it would be hard to equal another poem which, in its quintessentially British way, turns defeat into victory, tragedy into celebration. Loved by every British schoolboy, it rolls off the tongue as the mad British rolled into the cannonfire like so many coconuts in a shy:

Half a league, half a league,
Half a league onward,
All in the valley of Death
Rode the six hundred.
"Forward, the Light Brigade!
Charge for the guns!" he said:
Into the Valley of Death
Rode the six hundred.

"Was there a man dismayed?" asks Tennyson. Not so.
"Their's not to make reply, Their's not to reason why, Their's
but to do and die". It sounds like the urgings of every sergeant-
major to his raw recruits.

And so to the apotheosis, as the few left ride back again:

When can their glory fade?
O the wild charge they made!
All the world wondered.
Honour the charge they made!
Honour the Light Brigade,
Noble six hundred!

No schoolboy would be without that poem, or this — where
death is honoured in elegant and moving words, ennobling war
— always ennobling war:

Not a drum was heard, not a funeral note,
As his corpse to the rampart we hurried;
Not a soldier discharged his farewell shot
O'er the grave where our hero we buried.

Slowly and sadly we laid him down,
From the field of his fame fresh and gory;
We carved not a line, and we raised not a stone,
But we left him alone with his glory.
(Charles Wolfe: *The Burial of Sir John Moore*.)

To end, it seems fitting to go back in time, across the centuries
of bloodiest fields and mutilated men, to the 4th century BC
and China:

The warriors are all dead, they lie in the open fields.
They set out, but shall not enter; they went but shall not
    come back.

They fought so well — in death are warriors still;
Stubborn and steadfast to the end, they could not be
   dishonoured.
Their bodies perished in the fight; but the magic of their
   souls is strong —
Captains among the ghosts, heroes among the Dead!

Chapter 10
The Hero and Eternity

War has often been compared to a funfair. It is a good comparison. War is indeed like a giant carnival, all the fun of the fair, a prolongation of childhood games. There is just one small difference: in war, tanks no longer fire rubber pellets, and the target is not a cardboard cut-out, but a living soldier; the little boy, like a tree struck by lightning, lies prone, and will not rise again to carry on playing. This is not make-believe now. The burning factory really is on fire, and will not rise from its ashes. The battleship really is at the bottom of the ocean with all its crew, and will never surface. The corpse really is a corpse, and if circumstances permit, must be decently buried. So from that point of view, war really is a fair, the only circus worth the name, with death as the price for all, not just for the acrobats and the lion-tamers — but for the audience too.

Hence war's extraordinary power of attraction: war removes most brutally, deliciously, our mundane routine, the tedium of our existence. War breaks up the clockwork mechanism of our society and releases us from the pettiness and narrow security of the daily struggle. Bridges are burnt, there is a sense of adventure. Gone are stifling parents, shrewish wives, awkward lovers. Gone the monthly lack of funds, unpaid bills, tax increases, bank statements in the red. Gone the constant fear of bankruptcy, or of redundancy. No matter now questions of promotion, the jealousy of colleagues, the boss's bullying. Anxieties can be put to one side. The army takes over, and becomes mother and wife. The allowances and regular wages of conscripted men take care of family left behind. Better still soldiers are housed, fed and dressed for free; they have no need to spend money, and at last they can save up their earnings just as they always dreamt of doing, for the future — if they have any.

War teaches detachment from all things homely: soldiers in the field soon forget the look of a comfortable house with central heating, bathroom, soft beds. The very word comfort has disappeared from their vocabulary. They are free now from the life of ease and sloth which they never even knew was theirs. Free from the unnecessary delight they took in their nice little houses, monthly salaries, books, records, photo albums, children's drawings. The fighting man has no past. Nor does he have much of a future, which makes him suspended in time, outside time, cut off from the rest of the world, face to face with himself in his solitude. Previously, he never bothered to examine essential truths of life. Now that he is all alone, he can plumb the depths, find meaning to his existence.

That, at least, is what he should be doing, if it were not for the appalling promiscuity of life in the army, whether in the trenches or the dug-outs, back in headquarters or in the front line, in the heat of battle or in the PoW camp. Soldiers are pestered all the time. They cannot be alone, even for a second. They must live, eat, sleep, play and wash many to a room. The most basic digestive processes must be shared.

This life-style may be disastrous for exercising one's intellect and thought processes, but it brings about the most unbelievable transformation of the soldier's character and habits. Only yesterday he was fearful, shy, timid, worried about his health, fussy to the point of ridicule. He was a model of rectitude, his honesty proverbial, his manners beautiful, the most faithful of husbands. Now he is a new man. He eats with his fingers, he spits on the floor, he swears blind, gets drunk, rapes the servants, tells filthy stories, is messy, dirty, smelly, full of boasting and lies. He is unrecognisable. Yesterday he could not hurt a fly, today he is ready to wipe out the world's entire population. War has acted on him like a wonderful tonic, bringing out the highest virtues, the best qualities which perhaps otherwise never would have seen the light of day. War, in the words of Paul Bourget, is a means of regeneration.

A desire to live dangerously is the stuff of life. With the many extreme dangers which threatened our ancestors, they had no trouble satisfying that need. Today, these dangers have disappeared. Wild beasts are nowhere to be seen; thanks to weirs and dams, rivers hardly ever flood and when they do they can be controlled. What is left for lovers of strong sensations except for war?

It could be objected that nothing prevents anyone consumed by a death-wish to take up lion-taming, driving a racing car or becoming a trapeze artist. These jobs do carry with them a certain amount of risk — many a lion-tamer has lost an arm or a leg, a racing driver can misjudge a bend, or the acrobat his trapeze. Nevertheless these professions cannot be compared with soldiering. First, because they have been chosen, presumably with some care and a good deal of thought. Secondly, because the professional dare-devil is taking a calculated risk; lion-tamers get to know the danger signals and what is likely to infuriate their beasts; racing drivers know the maximum speeds they can reach without parting company with the road on a bend. A soldier, though, cannot assess the risk he is taking. He can only hope he will somehow get through the hail of bullets, and avoid the direct hit of a falling bomb from a plane passing overhead. It is virtually impossible for him to increase or lessen the risk. He is in the hands of chance, which of course is a relief to him. Finally, it must be said that the death of a racing driver is a great shock to all concerned, the death of a test pilot is tragic, the death of a lion-tamer dreadful. The death of a soldier, however, even if it occurs when he is running away, is always glorious.

This is why high risk in wartime has several advantages over the same amount of risk encountered in peaceful, but dangerous professions. And then on top of it all such risk is so much more democratic during war. No particular skill or talent is required. This makes it attainable by a large number of people, with the state's back-up for training and general support. War puts extreme dangers within reach of all men.

In war, the sort of exhilaration which always comes to those who dally with death is greatly heightened, fed as it is by a powerful mixture: the whine of bullets, the rifle's crack, the crump of shells. Fanfares, drums and bugles play their part. So do the groans of wounded men, the moans of the dying. Blood with its rich colour increases to frenzy the fighting man's excitement, in the same way that a wild animal will become a killer when it sees blood flow and smells it. Men attack each other ferociously, caught in the grip of the noblest of passions, and "the blood running on all sides serves only to encourage them to shed theirs and the enemy's. Men quickly become crazed as they carry out the carnage with joy in their hearts."[51]

It is worth noting that those who are most generous in shedding the blood of others are men whom old age or their position in the army protect from the machine gun. It is as if their enforced inactivity doubled their enthusiasm, which then expresses itself in burning exhortations which give them consolation.

Those who have fought in war agree that it is a unique source of happiness, and such is its power that it sweeps away anything which might resemble remorse. There are some famous examples of this. In his will, which he drew up on 29th April 1945, just before his suicide, Adolf Hitler — far from mourning the deaths of millions of young men he had sent to their graves — wrote this extraordinary sentence: "I die with a joyful heart."

The love of killing is one of the strongest emotions in existence. Anyone who has not sampled the delight of plunging a dagger into another man's heart, or mowing him down with a machine gun, has not known true pleasure. Curious about this human trait, philosophers have tried to analyse it, and some have put forward quite an interesting theory: when a man dies in battle, his strength passes into the body of his killer by a process which is little short of magical. A kind of transfusion, by which he then experiences a fullness and growth of power twenty times stronger than anything produced by a drug. Hence the descriptions fighting men give us of this condition which borders on the mystical: a passion in the soul, a serenity, an eruption of joy, flight of the spirit, ecstasy, love's rapture.

It is often assumed that war stokes up hatred between men. This is a mistake. Some rather cautious and timid people may need the spur of hatred to kill without compunction. The fact that they see before them a Commie or a Fascist Pig, makes the whole thing easier, freeing them from any scruples which might otherwise arise. But apart from these isolated cases, for most people "war is a page taken from the book of love."[52] Surprising as it may seem, to aim your rifle at a distracted enemy, to let fly a missile, bombard the opposing forces, spray them with automatic fire, tear them apart with shrapnel — these are gestures of love. The soldier who tosses a hand-grenade into a bunker where twenty enemy men are sheltering, does so with his heart overflowing with charity. What after all is the overriding emotion in this extract from Alexis Tolstoy's *Writings on War*? "The enemy planes buzzed around me like bees from the hive. My neck was aching from constantly swivelling my head round to see behind me. The excitement of the dogfight had overwhelmed me and I was shouting exultantly. Suddenly an enemy fighter is in my sights just below me. For a split second, the pilot is framed in the sights — a powerful and barbarous face, hatred in his eyes and fear too — the fear of one who wants to plead for his life. I fire. He somersaults, smoke pouring from his stricken machine." This surely backs up the maxim: "close encounters with the enemy are like a lover's touch."[53]

*   *   *

We have always heard that love transforms man: war, as an act of love, gives him his beauty. Maurice Barrès said enthusiastically of the French infantrymen of 1914: "How beautiful they are, defenders of our lives, in their trenches, behind their ramparts and their wire, digging, digging, at one with the soil of their nation!" This flattering and eulogising description, made by a great patriot some way away from the Front, is remarkably similar to the picture painted by the man on the spot: "We climbed and climbed. The men's faces were crimson. Their capes were open, their tunics undone, a handkerchief knotted round the throat, and their foreheads black with dirt and sweat which trickled in filthy rivulets from under their helmets, down the furrows of their suffering faces, onto their parched lips . . ."[54]

A soldier's good looks are attractive to women, especially as their admiration is tinged with understandable envy. The poor things are generally excluded from the fighting ranks, even though in recent years there has been some improvement in their situation. It is because she is not allowed to fire a gun that the woman finds herself in a state of inferiority to man, with her "intellectual characteristics of the savage: innate desire to show off, love of decorations, impulsive ways, disbelief of natural phenomena, religious mania, lack of general ideas."[55]

Stubborn but easily influenced, masochistically inclined, woman is invariably fatally attracted to soldiers and their uniforms, symbols of dominance and violence. In time of war, this feeling of attraction will be far stronger than in peacetime. A number of reasons for this exist. First, the surroundings facilitate adventures, with the black-out cloaking them in mystery and anonymity, stoking up curiosity. The constant movement of troops ensures a temporary quality to attachments, rather like the love affairs on a cruise ship or on holiday abroad. Hello, goodbye, together, apart, see you some time, probably never. A good experience. Between 1942 and 1945 two million illegitimate children were born in Italy.

It may also be that women have a natural desire to protect and care for men who have been selected for the ultimate sacrifice. Whatever the truth of it, there is a tangible link between the outbreak of war and a growth in sexuality, which historians have managed to prove. This is easily understood. Sex is made up of masochism and sadism, the same elements being found in the desire to fight. The masochistic need for sacrifice and self-destruction to be found in war becomes the desire to forget everything experienced in the ecstasy of sexual relations, a deep wish to faint away, described as a "little death". The sadistic pleasure of dominating others and hunting them as much as possible is to be found in love-making. Freud and others since have demonstrated that "the sexuality of most men contains elements of aggression." Even the apparently sublime desire to give a woman a child has elements of male sadism in it, revealing his need to keep her by him and possess her utterly. A jealous husband's first thought will invariably be to make his wife pregnant, to stop her flighty behaviour. The only difference between the sexual act and the desire for battle is that the former does not invariably end up with murder.

The slogan of 1968, "make love not war", is a nonsense. Love and war go together. Love is a form of war, with its ecstasy, its cruelty and its victims. It even borrows words from the language of war: we speak of love's quarrels, love's conquests, love's conflicts. Military vocabulary is extremely apt for love-making, as this extract from a German manual on the conduct of troops shows: "The more difficult an attack appears in advance, the more carefully must you prepare for it. Do not over-estimate the chances of success and thereby fail to provide sufficient backup. Do not work in haste as this may cause you to fail. Make use of the darkness to begin the operation, as an attack in the final hours of the night may enable you to disguise your intentions longer. If you meet little resistance in your first approach, go straight in with everything you have . . . but if resistance is fierce, prepare the assault with care . . . depending on how good your position is. Generally, every attack carried out in the face of strong opposition reaches a decisive moment. Immediately after the attack the adversary should be overwhelmed and the breach made permanent. If after the breakthrough you do not have the strength to continue, then it may be necessary to mark time in order to recuperate."[56]

*   *   *

A well-known fact is that a soldier is never tired. He can keep going until he drops — which he only does if someone puts a bullet in him. No truth whatsoever in stories about men "driven to breaking-point by levels of exhaustion never before experienced, their minds blank, heads heavy, bodies weighed down, a dreadful suffering permeating their limbs, all hope gone, joyless, like animals led quietly to the slaughter."[57] On the contrary, another writes: "the most exhausted men become the best fighters with a will to win."[58] Only when they have reached that ultimate state, when hunger gnaws at their entrails, when lack of sleep makes them into zombies, when fevers rack their bodies, do they display their finest qualities: lucid, quick, energetic, full of initiative, full of decision. Only their sense of humour lets them down, but that matters little: the army does not enjoy a high reputation for jocularity.

In peacetime, it is the courage of men and women who save life that is primarily recognised, such as surgeons, lifeboatmen, firemen, nurses. It is of no interest in war, because what really matters is the warrior's bravery, whose object is not to save life, but to take it.

Bravery in war, like common sense, is the best respected attribute, but it does no harm to stimulate it a little when it weakens. A ration of rum, say, or some other alcohol. Or a psychological spur: a quick pep talk, making it clear to the footsoldier that if he does not advance, he will certainly risk being shot from behind. Frederick the Great used to say that a soldier should be more frightened of his officers than of the enemy in order to fight well.

The fighting man can become frightened at any time, just as his stomach can fall out — often the former leads to the latter. Such fear is understandable, especially if it is his first battle, and it will invariably come to him there. Let him who has never experienced it fire the first shot!

Luckily for him and for his officers, it does die down gradually. So many bodies lie to the left, to the right, in front, behind, that in the end you cease to see them, or smell them, and you become hardened. Death becomes familiar.

In peacetime, a young man's death is tragic. In time of war, it is a daily and expected event. You share a joke with a friend, you offer him a cigarette, he holds out a hand to take it, he does not take it. He is dead. It is as simple as that — no need to make a song and dance about it. Death is no longer a dreadful parting, no longer does it involve a dramatic event, it no longer matters, has no particular value, makes no particular sense. It means nothing. Nor does life.

Soon there are more dead than alive on the Front, and this is awkward. A few white lies have to be told to set the record straight. It might be suitable, for instance, to pretend that the dead are not all really dead, and some of them are actually quite alive. Maurice Barrès, in another outburst of enthusiasm, declared: "O dead, how well you live on!" More alive than ever, someone else remarked. Another route is to assure people that the dead will actually stand up and form ranks to fill the gaps. This is particularly useful since, once dead, they can hardly be killed a second time, and so all the most dangerous tasks can safely be left in their hands. Lastly, with the survivors on the point of collapse, shell-shocked and battered, and unable to string two words together, then the dead are made to speak out. They are a safe enough bet: they will always say what is required in the wisest possible way. They reaffirm that "the nation is our strength, together we stand, God, for whom we sacrifice all, is our final consolation."[59] Since they have little to lose now, they call on the living to join them in "accepting with humble heart whatever privations are imposed on us." And as they are in no hurry, they call on their countrymen to "have patience, know how to await, calmly, the hour of deliverance."[60] No sign of revolt, no bitterness, no hint of regret, no word out of place, no breath of reproach for the High Command. Dead, they have become perfectly behaved.

The living have greater difficulties. It would be too easy to go along with the great troupe of authors, chroniclers, and war novelists who — to give themselves airs and justify a few nasty moments in their lives (and who has not had those?) — have given in to a desire for dramatisation, stuffing their works full of ghastly images and terrifying descriptions. Such items as: "a man bent in two, like a broken doll draped on the barbed wire, his head smashed and spilling out its contents slowly on the ground." Or then again: "smashed jaws, mutilated hands . . . other hands grasping a stomach to stop the entrails from bursting out, and eyes dilated with horror where death stares out at us as from a mask."[61] There are hundreds of examples — all, needless to say, gross exaggeration. The truth is altogether different, for from one end of the line to the other, the principal emotion is joy, the "laughter of the trenches, the laughter of the soldiers." It is our duty to sustain that hilarity with words of exhortation: "Go to it, you happy band — likely lads one and all! Be happy! Have fun! Dance! Laugh! Sing!"[62]

There may come a time when the fighting man's situation appears to get worse, when shells scream over the trenches, smashing into the living and the dead, flinging limbs everywhere, sending heads high in the air, emptying eyes from their sockets, making a bloody pulp of the flesh. At such times, he should be reminded that none of this is real but a disturbance of his imagination, that if he could but see it he is in the presence of the "cloistered calm of the cathedral"[63] and that war is nothing less than poetry in action.

*   *   *

People often say that the army is like one big family, and this is true. Just like a family, you have no choice about whom you are to live with. Circumstances decide — the haphazard movement of troops and organisation of fighting units. You and your comrades-in-arms are united by fear and suffering. There is no need for you to have likes and dislikes in common, a similar background and cultural upbringing. Whether you hit it off or whether you do not, for better, for worse especially, you are neighbours. In any case, why bother to forge close relationships with your army colleagues? Tomorrow, you may be posted elsewhere, or he will be wounded and transported to head-quarters, or you will be killed. In war, everything is temporary, friendship no exception.

Any family needs authority. The great military family needs it above all else. Discipline is the army's strength. There can be no question of a subordinate querying an order, arguing its merits — perish the thought! His first duty is to obey, to obey without hesitation, without question. An order is an order, even if it is idiotic. Once it has been carried out, and the pointless attack has been made with men killed, then he can complain to a senior officer; not that he has much hope of being listened to. The hierarchy will almost always protect the immediate superior, and the man lodging such a complaint will have his card marked from then on.

It has to work this way. If even one command is ignored, the entire structure may well collapse. This is why discipline is so vital to a High Command, and if there is any sign of laxity, draconian measures ensue. Guilty men are immediately despatched to the front line, or transferred to a squadron reserved for tough nuts, or more simply put in front of a firing squad. Needless to say, the latter solution is the one generally preferred by army chiefs.

Events moved too fast to make much use of it during the Second World War, but there were plenty of opportunities to do so during the First.

As the name implies, summary execution does not brook the delays involved in pleadings and other twists and turns of the law. If a trial takes place at all, then the whole thing takes minutes only. Rarely are there enquiries, depositions by witnesses, or statements from the accused. Often enough, his superior officer will make one or two discreet suggestions to the court martial panel, such as "best if we shoot him". Occasionally agreement is reached, the execution post ready, the grave dug, before the presiding officer has pronounced sentence.

Naturally this only happens in very serious cases, such as a soldier having an argument with his sergeant, which means he is moved to another regiment, he protests, his complaint is ignored, he makes a fuss, he is accused of "refusing to obey an order in the face of the enemy", and shot. Or, two men are told to take care of the kitbags of the soldiers going over the top; they are found guilty of desertion. Another infantryman gets drunk and is picked up by military police who accuse him of cowardice and give him the opportunity to sober up in Paradise. There is also the case of a soldier who refused to wear a dirty pair of trousers. He was shot, but he died in clean clothes.

Such casual justice inevitably got it wrong on occasion, but had the merit of always recognising an error and rehabilitating the numerous victims to whom this happened. The men in charge of the kitbags were reprieved — but only after they had been shot. Four French corporals who had been executed for failing to reach an unattainable objective were rehabilitated several years later and their widows received a nominal payment of one franc in compensation. Life was cheap in those days. As for the other French hero who refused to wear dirty trousers, he

was shot in 1915, rehabilitated in 1922, and the colonel who had
him executed was promoted general and received the Legion of
Honour, Commander grade. He deserved it.

No fewer than two thousand innocent people were executed
between 1914 and 1918. Why be sorry it happened to them —
their guilt or lack of it was not the point; the important thing was
to set an example.

*   *   *

Bravery provokes an extraordinary rush of adrenalin. It is much
like anger: the combatant sees red, no longer knows what he is
doing, "is lifted up and carried along on the wings of a mighty
impulse which brooks no resistance".[64] He experiences a
special trembling of the body which chimpanzees know as the
forerunner of battle against a fellow creature. The only
difference is that he cannot use it, unlike the chimp, to make his
hair stand on end.

The battle over, he becomes master of his emotions again —
assuming he is still alive. This is a dangerous moment. He just
could start to think, and that is why it is so necessary for his
superiors to ensure he does not fall into that temptation. The
entire success of their operation depends on it. It is not easy,
after all, to send millions of people to their death without any
kind of resistance on their part. They have to be pretty well
conditioned for the system to function so smoothly. And it does
function, with few hiccoughs. Mutiny is a very rare phenomenon.
This is little short of miraculous.

It is a commanding officer's job to persuade a private that
displaying intelligence will do him no good, bringing with it
troubles and disillusionment. Thinking, he will point out, gives
you wrong ideas. No need for him to try to get at the truth, as
that is already being done for him by his superiors, who can see
more clearly than he can.

Should he persist in using his brain the authorities will
convince him that in any case he would not understand war, it
being a mysterious, almost occult phenomenon, with its own
impetus bearing it out of our control, and whose ultimate goal is
to be found "well beyond any influence of human reason".[65]

*   *   *

A soldier's behaviour must be akin to that of the rat: gentle and understanding towards the members of his own group, cruel and ferocious towards every stranger. Lose this delicate balance, tip the scales the other way, and disaster threatens. The war machine, till now well oiled, starts to grind to a halt. One word is repeated from mouth to mouth in headquarters, and it strikes terror in the hearts of the generals: fraternisation.

This is a very special psychological disease. The poor victim can no longer distinguish between the person next to him, and the one opposite. So troubled is he that — as though their uniforms had fallen from their bodies — he can no longer see anything other than two naked men, just like him, two poor sods, two brothers in suffering, ready to shake hands.

Moreover, this illness — being contagious — could spread like wildfire with the most appalling consequences: combatants on both sides throwing down their weapons, coming together not to kill each other but to join forces against their leaders, the military hierarchy, which then collapses, its officers in flight, the war brought to a sudden halt.

Luckily for us, the fraternisation bug only breeds in a rare atmosphere. It needs many long months of bloody battles, weakening body and spirits, as happened in 1917. The authorities have learnt how to cope with this sickness, the simplest method being the surgical one of cutting it out of the system.

Preventive medicine is also important, which means maintaining the enemy's image as a hideous creature to be destroyed without delay. It becomes important to impede the dissemination of any reports which might indicate that he has feeling, that he cares for someone, that he believes in God, that he can be charitable, that he too has doubts, that he can be depressed like the rest of us.

Thus protected and immunised against his environment, a soldier can continue to fight. His spirit free, his head empty, his imagination dead, his mental processes shut down. He does not know, he must never know, that at the precise moment when he is writing to his mother, his wife or his fiancée, hundreds of other men of all races, in all climates, wearing every kind of uniform, are scribbling much the same words on their bits of paper . . .

MARC TO GERMAINE: "The photos I received recently are

my closest companions. Twenty times a day I pull them out of my wallet and look at them."

> *Marc Boasson, killed 29 April 1918.*

FRITZ TO BARBARA: "Yet again, I took your photograph in my hands and stared at it for a long time. It spoke to me of that moment we spent together on that lovely summer evening in the last year of peace, when we were walking towards our house through a carpet of flowers."

> *One of the Stalingrad letters confiscated by the German High Command for reasons of morale.*

KIYOSHI TO HIS FAMILY: "So many thoughts cross my mind. Student life in Tokyo this time last year. My warm bed, hot soup, my desk bathed in sunlight, the smell of printer's ink from the newspapers left on the chair . . ."

> *Kiyoshi Takeda, 22, killed April 1945.*

ERNST TO HIS FAMILY: "Peace! All the nostalgia which possesses us when we are separated from our loved ones for so long, everything we desire for ourselves, every dream of the future which haunts us in the trenches, all of it enclosed in this one word, such a gentle word: peace."

> *Ernst Hieber, killed five days after writing this letter, 11 April 1915.*
> *A student of theology.*

MAURICE TO HIS PARENTS: "I have seen too many disgusting things to believe in certain words which impress ignorant or naive people. Why are we fighting this war, why now, and in this particular way? Whom are we trying to save? What are we defending, and what are we trying to win?"

> *Maurice Genevoix. Letter written March 1915.*

LUDWIG TO HIS FAMILY: "We are told we are fighting for Germany, but not many of us believe that our sacrifice will do the nation any good."

> *Letter from Stalingrad.*

JOE TO HIS MOTHER: "My dear Mother, I thought that war was a glorious adventure, but what a mistake I made. It's just hell with the lid off . . . What awful thing have I let myself in for? Surely God never meant his creatures to settle quarrels in this way. We must live and act like beasts. It is terrible! . . . I am young, but I feel old. I have lived a hundred years in a week."

Three months earlier this young volunteer, known in his memoirs as Bombardier X, wrote some rather different letters to his mother from Scotland, before leaving for the Western Front: "Well, I'm in the Army at last, Mother dear, and I feel ever so happy . . . The Colonel made a wonderful speech when he asked for volunteers. He said that the future of England was in our hands. We, the youth of England, must step forward and offer to our country what it required. I was ever so proud when he shook me by the hand for stepping forward. He said how he envied me for my youth and the chance that was mine to earn glory. To be addressed like that by a Colonel would make any boy proud. My heart feels as if it's singing, and my flesh is tingling. At last I'm going to see life and adventure. My country needs me. After all, I am sixteen . . . How proud you'll be when your boy takes his place among men in the fighting line . . . How I long to see big guns spit fire, and to feel them quiver under my hand as they hurl death at our enemies!"

Then in April 1915 he arrived at Le Havre and had his first contact with veterans: "France is no longer a dream. I am here, on the doorstep of the battlefield. I rub shoulders with men who were in the trenches yesterday . . . They tell us stories. They are awful tales, but they can't be true. I must get there quickly to see for myself."

KONRAD TO HIS FATHER: "I sought God in every shell-hole, every burnt-out house, on every street corner, with every comrade, when I was hiding in a trench — even in the sky above . . . God never revealed Himself, even though my soul cried out in anguish for Him . . . Father, God does not exist! Or if He does, then He is to be found in prayer books and hymns, in pious sermons from holy priests, in the tolling of the bell and the smell of incense, but not in Stalingrad."

Letter from Stalingrad.

ARTHUR TO A FRIEND: "For the Hun I feel nothing but a spirit of amiable fraternity that the poor man has to sit just like us and do all the horrible and useless things that we do, when he might be at home with his wife or his books, as he preferred."

Captain Arthur Graeme West, 26, killed 3 April 1917.

MARC TO HIS WIFE: "They came to fetch me . . . to question some Hun prisoners . . . a twenty-year-old lieutenant. Twenty

— he looked seventeen! Just a kid, pale, thin, scared eyes like a gazelle's in a narrow white face . . . When I entered, he fixed his eyes on me and I tried to read his thoughts there. What would I find in that enemy mind? Enemy! . . . A pathetic hero, a shopkeeper, a peace-loving child, sometimes tender, often docile, remembering his lessons about sacrifice for your country just as he would remember, as a good pupil, his lessons in maths and history."

Marc Boasson.

KARL TO HIS FAMILY: "I supervised the burial of two Frenchmen . . . and took their papers. There were letters from their families . . . One from a woman who always ended with the words: 'Baby is always good.' One, a sister writing to her brother that she is sending him two pounds of chocolate; she also promises him some gloves to keep out the damp and a hood to guard against the rain. No different from our own, and as I read them I can feel the last spark of hatred of the French going out — always assuming it was still there."

Karl Iosenhaus, killed 25 January 1915. Student of theology.

ROBERT TO HIS WIFE: "A German falls a hundred yards from me, his head smashed by a bullet. He had no time to defend himself. One enemy less, but how many tears will flow tomorrow perhaps, how many hearts will be broken, because a loved one is no more! . . . I must love my country, but that is no reason for hating others and dreaming of nothing but slaughter . . . Faced with such physical suffering, one forgets the facile hatreds of war, and it is brought home how much we are all one, only too mortal flesh!"

Captain Robert Dubarle, killed 15 June 1915.

BERNHARD TO HIS FAMILY: "An American pilot comes down by parachute, his plane in flames. He breaks his right leg and he's there without movement in a field covered in snow. I am the first to reach him. He is scared he is going to be shot out of hand. As best we can, we make a splint and carry him back . . . Full of gratitude, he shakes my hand. How easily we could understand each other — how true it is! We must remain enemies just because we live in different countries."

Bernhard Beckering, killed 25 January 1945.

PIERRE TO LOUISE: "I woke on a sudden one night, and I thought I saw a German I'd killed flying into the air. I could hear him screaming . . . It came to me that the poor sod probably had a wife like me, who wouldn't see him again, that he probably had a boy like Emile and maybe a little girl like Marguerite, like me. I never once trembled when the bullets and shells whined over my head, but that night I wept for shame."

Pierre Castagné, killed 4 February 1916.

RENÉ TO HIS MOTHER: "My dearest Mother, if you receive this letter, then I will have been killed . . . I will have died carrying out my duty as you taught me to do from a young age . . . I was enjoying living and would have liked to continue. But Fate decided otherwise . . . I hope that my death will serve a purpose . . . I hope that an allied victory frees us forever from the horrors of war . . . Only poets, historians and journalists find beauty in war."

René Carbonnel, killed 16 April 1917.

FRIEDRICH TO HIS SISTER: "Hermann has just received your letter telling us the news of the death of Mum and Dad . . . It's a good thing I think that they will never know now that Hermann and I will never return . . . I would have liked to be a theologian, Dad wanted a small house, and Hermann wanted to drill wells. None of it happened . . . Our parents are lying under the rubble of their house, and as for us, tough as it may seem, we are dug in along with about a hundred of our mates in a ravine . . . Soon the snow will come to fill it up . . ."

Letter from Stalingrad.

WILFRID TO HIS PARENTS: "No-one can make me believe now that our comrades' dying words are 'Germany' or 'Heil Hitler!' . . . Their last words are for their mothers, for a loved one, or a cry for help."

Letter from Stalingrad.

ICHIZO TO HIS MOTHER: "Mother, the time has come for me to give you some very sad news . . . In two days I shall be leaving, in two days I shall be dead . . . Mother, you wanted me to have a brilliant career, and I am going to disappoint you. I will never forget how worried you were when I was taking my exams. I joined this group (kamikaze pilots) against your wishes . . . I admit now that I would have done better to follow your advice . . . When I think that I will never see you again, I become mad with sorrow . . ."

Ichizo Hayashi, 23, killed at Okinawa.

GEORG TO HIS FATHER: "Tomorrow, I shall cross the last bridge, which is a poetic way of describing death . . . Hold my hand, so the road may be less hard . . . We have come to the end. We may be able to hold out for eight days, but no more . . . You can rest assured it will all happen in a dignified manner. It's a bit early for my thirtieth birthday yet, I know. Let's not be sentimental. Say hello to Lydia and Helene, kisses to Mother (be careful, don't forget her weak heart). Kiss Gerda for me. My best wishes to everyone else. Father, the lieutenant salutes you and begs to be dismissed."

Letter from Stalingrad.

RUDOLPH TO HIS FATHER, a German Army general: "The moment is coming when every thinking German will curse the madness of this war, and you will know what a hollow ring the word 'flag' has, which was once our inspiration for victory . . . There is no victory, General. Still flags and men fall, until at the end no flags and no soldiers will be left."

Letter from Stalingrad.

HEINRICH TO A FRIEND: "What has all this to do with me? . . . What is it to us, companions of a living hell? What the f . . . does this death of a hero mean to me? Death must always be heroic and joyful. We must always die with conviction, for a good cause. And the truth of it here? . . . Men fall like flies, with no-one caring for them, without arms or eyes, stomachs, full of holes . . . It would make a great film — imagine: 'The finest death in the world'. More like the death of cattle in the slaughter-house, later to be turned into the Death of a Warrior sculpted in granite, his head bandaged or his arm in a sling . . . Novels will be written, hymns sung, oratorios composed, masses said . . ."

Letter from Stalingrad.

*   *   *

Despite his regrettable bitterness, this young German, killed on the Russian Front in 1943, was perceptive enough. There is no need to carry out some great feat of arms to be called a hero. War is like one of those children's games where each player wins a prize. A generous nation hands out certificates of heroism to each participant, dead or alive. The former have the best part to play, of course. They are definitive heroes in an unchanging role, with a right to their names on a monument, remembrance ceremonies and *Te Deums* till the cows come home. The survivors do not fare so badly either. With little expense, the State supplies them with citations and congratulations, covers them in medals and ribbons, and organises on their behalf plenty of gatherings to keep alive the eternal flame which threatens at every moment to go out.

Gradually, the lowly private who had found himself projected into the battle without any clear idea why, ends up believing that he is a man of renown. On Sundays he proudly shows his grandchildren his bayonet, still stained with blood, and which he keeps like a sacred relic. That in itself shows that killing your fellow-men in battle is not murder, otherwise like the assassin he would throw the instrument of the crime away. For the rest of his life he will bore his listeners with those legendary months of his life at war, months which were actually spent cowering in a trench, terrified out of his wits, waist high in mud and filth.

Filled with self-glorification, he eventually comes to believe by an inevitable process that he served in a great cause. He never stops to think that the laurels bestowed on him, far from being a genuine gesture for him alone, are really aimed at firing the nation's patriotism. He is strong in the belief that he saved his country from the stranger's yoke, that he safeguarded our freedom, that he 'did his bit' to prevent new wars.

The fact is that he can see no further than the end of his rifle, and what he fails to realise is that man's freedom is as much at risk as ever, or worse; yesterday's enemy, whom he tried so hard to wipe out on two occasions, is today's friend; one of his allies, whom he supported so vociferously, may well become the next enemy; and the 'war to end war' was just an empty slogan.

Happy man, with his private dreams. Do not wake him. He is better off that way. Why should he be made to understand that his suffering, his hopes and his sacrifices were useless, and his friends all died for nothing?

Epilogue

A few years ago the administrations of a number of psychiatric hospitals in America embarked on an experiment to allow their patients to have a say in the running of their institutions. A university professor was given permission to make a study of the result. The worthy man could not believe his eyes. There were four times as many manic depressives or paranoid schizophrenics suffering from delusions of grandeur or persecution mania among those who had sought positions of responsibility than among the rest of the patients.

The professor came to an immediate and damning conclusion: namely, that world leaders inevitably suffered from paranoid tendencies. Hence the widespread existence of certain ailments among political and military leaders: mental sclerosis, inflexibility, suspicion and a serious inability to accept new attitudes. Suspicion breeds paranoia, where the sufferer believes his neighbour to be more hostile than he is himself, in other words, he sees him through a grille which eliminates any possibility of good will or openness.

Come an intellectual crisis, and political and military leaders are clearly less able to evaluate the facts lucidly, to anticipate their consequences, to arrive at sensible solutions to the problems, in short to make proper decisions, since they are bound to panic because of their pathological state. To quote Professor J.R. Raser: "Even in the thick of warfare, man may become a self-destroying misfit."

Were all the above true, it would be worrying. Logically, it would be enough to give us a few shivers in the spine, knowing that the manic depressives in charge of our security lose control at the slightest hitch, and aware that the men in charge of the nuclear button are uncontrolled megalomaniacs.

Nothing of the sort is the case, naturally. On the contrary, the men and women shaping the destinies of nations display a breadth of vision, a suppleness and creative flair that are amazing. The moment a dramatic situation confronts them,

these innovators show a talent for improvisation and turn the
world on its head with their brilliant ideas, putting forward
revolutionary proposals which set the people aflame with
enthusiasm, rallying the most pessimistic, appealing to the thirst
for idealism of the younger generation. At last, a generous
proposal, broader horizons, a new language! At last, tough
talking so long awaited! "The defence budget will increase by
5%. The production of new missiles will be stepped up.
Research on new armaments will be intensified." Is this not
heady stuff?

*   *   *

It would not be right to end this study without giving some idea
of what the future might hold in store. It is the reader's right to
know how his doom might come about. The nuclear arsenal,
impressive vanguard of our armies though it might be, should
not make us lose sight of other, less fashionable weapons, which
might hold a few surprises.

Gas was not used in the last world war. Not, obviously, for
humanitarian reasons, or for lack of supplies. On the contrary,
every protagonist was ready to make war with chemical
weapons, and only tactical considerations prevented them. This
should not lead us to despair or to conclude that such weapons
have no future. In any case, chemical agents were used by the
Italians in Ethiopia in 1936, by the Japanese against China in
1941, and by the Egyptians in the Yemen in 1966 and 1967 and
in the current ongoing conflict between Iraq and Iran.

Everyone knows too that the Americans made extensive use
of herbicides and pesticides in Vietnam, thus introducing some
variety in nature's monotonous cycle, upsetting the ecological
equilibrium and producing still-born foetuses or deformed
children. Satisfactory too were the various gases which made not
just the enemy cry, but sometimes his widow too, in particular
one which in concentrated doses produces lesions in the lungs
which can often prove fatal. In all likelihood, the Viet Cong did
not take very long to organise similar deliveries to the
Americans.

Since the good old days of phosgene gas, much progress has
been made. Between 1914 and 1918, only some 800,000 men
were killed by poison gas. In 1936 a German chemist, engaged
in research to find a gas which would eliminate certain insects,

found one instead which would do the same for human beings. This, the first gas to cause general paralysis, led to the discovery of another, and by 1944 of yet another, thirty times more potent than chlorine gas.

Paralysing or neurotoxic gases have a number of advantages. They are odourless and colourless, and equally effective employed as gases or sprayed under pressure. They get into clothes, working very fast with spectacular results. The victim's sight goes, his nose runs, his breathing becomes laboured, his bowels loosen, his muscles contract, and death through asphyxia ensues. Forty drops of this poison on a soldier's uniform have a fifty percent chance of killing him.

To the joy of the scientists, such toxic agents have enormous power, but this makes them difficult to handle. Chemists have found a way round this problem: a number of projectiles such as bombs, rockets, naval shells and intercontinental missiles are fitted with two separate and individually harmless substances, which turn into a lethal gas only when they have safely arrived at their destination, well away from the sender. These gases, known as binary, which carry no risk to their originators, have brought about a renewal of interest in gas warfare in military HQs. Production is at full stretch. In the United States, as in the Soviet Union, dozens of factories are working overtime, and new ones are being constantly set up. Present-day and future agreements are hypocritical of course, as civil and military technology are precisely the same. Actual stocks of the two super-powers are thought to amount to more than 100,000 tonnes. France, it should be noted, is the only Western European nation which possesses major reserves, and concerning world research she is comfortably in credit, with plenty of assistance from the United States, in particular over university research as well as industry. Thanks to the determination of her scientists, she has managed to create both a system of detection and one of defence, as well as further, more lethal gases.

Detection is achieved by means of an infra-red radar system which allows identification of the gas and evaluation of its concentration. Defence against it is achieved by using belladonna and atropine. Speed is of the essence, and armed forces working on operations where chemical weapons may be used have a small automatic injector fixed to their thighs and full of atropine. Even groggy from the effects of gas, a man still has the strength to push the button to inject himself. There are some five million doses already prepared in Britain and the USA. During the Six-Day War, Israeli soldiers carried this equipment.

Other, unexplored paths have been opened up by research. British scientists have founded a dreadful dynasty, known as V agents. VX is so powerful that cyanide seems positively beneficial in comparison. The Americans have perfected BZ, which is so lethal that the merest hint of it is enough to finish you off: loss of memory, hallucinations, loss of sense of orientation, gradual loss of all co-ordination. Another, ten times more powerful, is apparently under lock and key in a French establishment. In every case, the required lethal dose gets smaller, until eventually, the tiniest drop on the skin is enough to despatch you to the hereafter. Perhaps in the end, instead of Fly-Tox, we will be able to buy across the counter Man-Tox, in economy size and handy pocket size.

*   *   *

Biological warfare can have its own grandeur. In 600 BC, the enemies of the Athenians had to surrender, not through force of arms, but because of the terrible diarrhoea which had swept through their ranks. The Athenians had doctored the river the enemy were using for their water supply. Four hundred years later an enterprising Carthaginian pretended to flee with his army and abandoned his camp. He had taken the precaution of leaving behind a large stock of wine treated with mandragora. Naturally the enemy's troops drank it, and fell asleep. He came back and was able to massacre them at will. It was current practice during the Crusades to put corpses infected with plague into the enemy camp. This was not often necessary, though, as nature would frequently take charge and decimate armies with diseases far more lethal than mere weapons. In 1763 the British commander-in-chief in America, Sir Jeffrey Ambert, sent a goodwill present to the Indian Chiefs in a splendidly chivalrous gesture. He did forget to tell them, though, that the two blankets and the handkerchief which he had obtained from a British hospital were contaminated. The smallpox epidemic which followed saved him the unpleasant task of killing the Indians with guns. Systematic pollution of water reservoirs, springs and wells have almost always been carried out in conflicts from earliest times. Such practices, though, are the merest hints of what could be done and what is now in the mind of military leaders, though unfortunately, it has not yet had an opportunity to reveal itself.

The best diseases to propagate, the experts would have us believe, are the plague, cholera, tuberculosis and an interesting ailment called melioïdosis, which produces schizophrenia and delirium, as well as having the great advantage of being resistant to most antibiotics. Midway between chemical substances and bacteria are the toxins, in particular Botulism A. In ideal circumstances a dosage lethal to man is approximately $0 \cdot 12$ microgrammes, or 1,200 millionths of a gramme. It has been calculated that 250 grammes of botulism toxin placed in the reservoir of a town with a population of 250,000 inhabitants would be enough to wipe out the entire population in twenty-four hours. It is an extraordinary thought. Naturally, circumstances are rarely ideal, and the amount needed would probably be higher. Nevertheless, military men are practical, and they would not waste their time on biological warfare if the idea were not feasible. They do not pursue schemes without a good reason, even if they do sometimes waste astronomic amounts of money on plans which never see the light of day. The proof is that the factories, the laboratories, the bacillae which ask only to reproduce themselves, are all real.

Biological warfare is very tempting. It leaves buildings alone — factories, bridges, railways etc. — and destroys only people. The cultures are cost-effective, and their use extremely cheap. No sophisticated missiles, just a few drops in a reservoir; or a box parachuted from an aeroplane at the dead of night and opening on the ground to release its deadly cargo of plague-infested rats; or mosquitoes infected with yellow-fever, or flies carrying cholera.

It would be dishonest to maintain that there is no risk. The contaminated mammals or insects may adapt badly to their environment and die. Conversely, the disease may develop uncontrollably and wipe all humanity off the face of the earth. The enemy too, may be able to detect the imminence of an attack, thanks to a very careful vigilance, despite such means of detection as fluorescent antibodies still being experimental; he can then vaccinate his troops against the most likely viruses. Automatic injectors can carry out some seven hundred injections an hour.

An American admiral wrote: "We must convince the

scientific community that biological and chemical warfare are not dirty, and they are no worse than any other way of killing masses of people."[66] He was right, of course. Only the most stubborn and absurd prejudices would make us think these weapons are inhuman. What is the difference between death by asphyxiation, by radioactivity, by bullet or by the plague? There is none, so much so that we may pass from chemical war to bacteriological war without difficulty, by means of step-by-step reprisals: from CS gas in all its innocence to paralysing gases, then to toxins, and finally to bacteria and viruses. The result is every bit as good as with nuclear war.

Even though the authorities tend to be less generous with their information than they are concerning the atom bomb, it is known that a bomber carrying a load of neuro-toxic gas would kill at least a third of the population in an area of some one hundred square miles; if the load was a biological weapon, the death rate would amount to at least half the population.

*   *   *

Some people take pleasure in saying that army chiefs have acquired 'intelligent' weapons to compensate for their own slight lack of grey matter. This is absolutely not so. They are very intelligent and prove it by making such good use of scientific discoveries. For some years now the new micro-technology has become a vital part of our weaponry. We have ultra-precision guidance equipment, computerised to pinpoint targets, including a radar system which can zero in on 4,500 targets at once. Cruise missiles have a memory map, and a device on board provides a complementary relief map of the actual position, enabling them to adjust their flight paths. Ground-to-ground missiles are the darlings of the artillery, with their very own capability to seek out a programmed target such as the engine of a tank. Others come down by parachute and thanks to their acoustic sensors can detect the exact nature of the approaching enemy and deal with him accordingly.

The creation of robots and miniaturisation go hand in hand. Weapons are becoming more refined and discreet. Nuclear arms entered the panoply with no great fuss. Even the neutron bomb, which for some time was headline news, and was universally condemned, is now being manufactured on the quiet. To be sure, Cruise and Trident have recently come under attack from the anti-nuclear body, but they are being installed nevertheless. It is perfectly logical: no weapon is ever abandoned, given that it works efficiently. Hence the interest in that beautiful weapon the neutron bomb, since it can wipe out the occupants of tanks and leave the vehicle in one piece for subsequent re-use. The shell is intact, the animal inside it dead. Perfect.

The bottom of the sea has not been forgotten. Thousands of hydroplanes fixed to the seabed catch every sound, every unusual movement of the sea. It is said that they are able to locate a submarine within five miles. More information is gleaned from buoys sensitive to sound and dropped from aeroplanes, from instruments to measure magnetic fields, infra-red sensors, lasers and so on. Even the tiniest lift in temperature of sea-water resulting from the presence of a submarine can be detected by such sensors. It is a terrible thought — but what would happen to all these grown-up children with their headsets, their screens, their microphones, their buttons, their war-games played day and night — what would become of their international surveillance mounted round-the-clock, were there to be agreement on disarmament?

There is little risk, and the game of hide-and-seek will continue.

There is another weapon, infrequently mentioned, but not neglected for all that. It concerns meteorological warfare, and the experts question whether it would be possible to bring about monsoon rains at will, or disastrous hail-storms, or bolts of lightning or erupting volcanoes. In August 1975, it was agreed that such activities should be banned, but the wording of the agreement was so vague as to mean nothing.

To end on a happier note: three different strands of research are in progress. First, there is the use of ultrasound to destroy blood globules, but without any noise at all, which should please the noise abatement people. Then there is the ubiquitous gamma ray, which goes through metal three feet thick like a knife through butter, and which can also explode blood globules, as well as making certain of its victims by paralysing them. Finally, there is the possibility of an electro-magnetic ray which would be pitched at the same frequency as the human heart. The merest hint of this delightful weapon's force would be enough to pull the victim's heart into sympathetic resonance with the emission's frequency and it would be cooked to a turn.

*   *   *

The worldwide stockpile of nuclear arms, which as everyone knows is meant to avert the ultimate holocaust, is now estimated to total 100,000 megatons. That amounts to more than twenty tons of TNT per head, man, woman and child, for the entire world. As it happens, one pound of explosive is enough to kill a human being, which means we have a very decent surplus for our security. So what would be the effects if — as a growing number of experts seem to be hoping — a nuclear war broke out all over the world tomorrow?

Every media newsroom, every committee on world affairs has been a venue for exploring this question. The war game is popular, and the number of dead is anybody's guess. Taking a conservative view to begin with: following a nuclear attack on economic and military targets in an enemy country, total: 100 million dead. Do I hear 150 million? 180 million? Once, twice, for the third time, sold at 200 million dead.

It is generally agreed that the most likely situation is one where all-out nuclear war occurs following either military escalation or 'to end it all', where tension has mounted to intolerable levels: but that does not completely rule out the danger of an accident. Several occasions have already occurred when this might have come about. No one can forget the atomic bomb which had to be salvaged from the sea just off the coast of Spain. Another incident received less publicity: on 24th January 1961, a B52 bomber carrying two nuclear warheads of 24 megatons each, caught fire and crashed. One of the warheads was released on a parachute but the other hit the ground still on the plane. Subsequent examination showed that out of four systems of safety on the bomb, two had failed. 24 megatons is equivalent to 1,330 times the power of the bomb on Hiroshima . . . It must be remembered that the danger of such an incident rises in direct relation to the increasing number of bombers using the skies, and equipped with their deadly weaponry.

A few years ago there was considerable controversy in academic circles in the USA over another issue related to this problem. A professor from the University of Chicago stated that an H bomb exploding deep in the sea would set off a chain reaction which nothing would be able to stop, owing to the high pressure on the sea bed, and the hydrogen content of the deep. Considering the fact that two submarines have already had accidents at sea and sunk to the bottom with their nuclear arsenals intact, questions should be asked.

Though the possibility of such an accident remains, it is unlikely, and we may be better employed in other considerations. The best path to take is that shown us by Hermann Kahn, the American specialist. He points out that we possess not only the theoretical knowledge, but the industrial capability to bring the hour of reckoning closer. It is now in our power to build a machine which would represent the ultimate in the continuing arms race, the logical outcome of defence by nuclear deterrent. This weapon has no known defence against its might, no missile or satellite, laser or other system of interception, which puts it beyond any negotiation, threats or reprisals. It entails suicide for the nation that launches it, as well as total destruction of the rest of the world. The Americans have named it, flippantly, 'the Doomsday machine'. At today's prices, it costs about 100 billion dollars, and it is the last word in scientific progress.

*   *   *

Man's disappearance off the face of the earth is no longer an impossible dream, whether it is achieved by warfare planned in advance, or by accident, suicidal and grandiose or through human error. No-one seems tormented by this, begging for a little more time, complaining there is so much left to be done to improve man's lot. Who is going to believe anyone who makes that point? Why should we do better second time round, since we failed over four thousand years? Let us face it, our record is pathetic. We have not managed to overcome injustice, poverty, or violence. Brotherhood, tolerance and love did not triumph. We were not even able to feed the world's inhabitants, thousands of them still dying of hunger every day. And still we ask for another chance.

It would be more honest to examine man's pride and his insignificance. Our attitude to nature has been to conquer it. Bereft of natural weapons, we created some. Once we had overcome the animals, we started on each other, forgetting our lack of instinctive mechanism to prevent us from destroying ourselves. Now, too late, it seems, to save ourselves, we are caught in the wheel like cogs. We have come to the end of the road, and perhaps that is why we have been able to discover a weapon to bring the world to an end.

Whatever the truth of it all, the spectacle is worth watching. The box office is now open for the last night, with its traditional parade of all the troupe, singers, acrobats, clowns, trapeze artists, jugglers and fortune tellers, here to say their last goodbyes. A brilliant spotlight focuses on the ring, a tremendous clap of thunder shakes the stage props, and man's great adventure, his bloody history, his illusions and hopes, the earth with its cities, its streets, its cars, its gardens, its factories and tiny houses with minute little people hurrying about inside them, all of it in a split second roars into flame, explodes into a million fragments, is blasted into oblivion, leaving little more than a cloud of dust and matter which gradually disperses into nothing, vanishing into the great ether, absorbed by the countless stars into their eternal silence.

Appendix I
A Chronology of War

A simple chronology of principal wars from the 28th century BC to the present day.

2730 BC: King Oudemon launches a surprise attack across the Delta. 2690 BC: King Smerket imitates him and strikes at Sinai (which has seen little peace since). 2200 BC: Chaldea is invaded by the kings of Elam. 1800 BC approximately: the Hittites hit Cappadocia. Fifty years later, Babylon falls, followed by wars in Egypt and Libya, Philistines against Hebrews, Hebrews against Arameans, Assyrians against Syrians. It all gets rather confusing.

770 BC: Western Chinese conquer the Mongols. 732 BC: Teglath-Phalasar knocks a few heads about. 721 BC: Israel is destroyed. 650 BC: Babylon again, not for the last time.

Scythians, Medes, Spartans, Macedonians fight for every inch of territory, taking and retaking towns, butchering each other with great enthusiasm. Battle follows battle. 600 BC: first religious war. 480 BC: Thermopylae. 457 BC: Tanagra. Punic Wars set in, Carthage versus Rome, until Carthage is finally razed to the ground in 149 BC.

Rome does not have time for a breather. War has broken out with Mithridates who has just destroyed the Scythians. 66 BC: Pompey sorts things out and seizes Jerusalem. 58 BC: Caesar fights the Helvetians in Gaul and defeats Vercingetorix. There follows several hundred years of Roman warring.

238 AD: the Goths cross the Danube for the first time, and they set off three hundred years of barbarian invasions — Visigoths, Goths, Vandals and Huns spread across Europe and the Middle-East, killing, raping, burning, laying waste and pillaging everything in sight.

638: the Arabs take Jerusalem and Antioch. Islam begins its reign. They enter Egypt, India, almost the whole of Spain. They join forces with Tibet against China (736) and beat the latter (751), they join forces with China against Tibet (798) but their decline starts in 800, while the Franks begin their ascendance, fighting Saxons, Saracens and Greeks.

The Normans, the Norwegians and the Danes come next, and they make their mark. Meanwhile the Slavs do battle in Germany, the Hungarians devastate Italy, Iraq suffers a barbarian invasion and Pope John X pulverises the infidels. Not forgetting to set an example, the Supreme Pontiff is assassinated in 928, thus fulfilling the prophecy in the New Testament that he who lives by the sword shall die by the sword.

The new millenium opens with more massacres and the spectacular invasion of England by Normandy in 1066.

There follow many years of holy Crusades, enabling Christians to sort out a few infidels. In 1095 the Crusaders reach Constantinople, and in 1099 they take Jerusalem. Others continue the action too, and there is little peace in Africa or Europe. Empires are founded and ruined like packs of cards: from Roman to Christian, Byzantine to Arab, Frank to Mongol. The latter devastate northern China, Eastern Europe, Turkey and much of the Far East. Later battles ensue between France and England, between Christians and Infidels again, back to western Europe with the start of the Hundred Years War and great victories (and defeats) on both sides: Crecy, Calais, Poitiérs, Limoges, Orléans, Joan of Arc, Formigny, Castillon — names that straddle the middle of the fifteenth century. Plenty of marshalls, dukes, princes, pirates and bandits continue their various warring activities around the world. There is fighting in Armenia, India, England again, Hungary, Poland of course, Siam. In 1485, Russian and Swedish armies hammer it out in Finland. In 1494, the French fight in Italy. Everlasting peace is established after the great battle of Marignan in 1515. It ends in 1521 when Francis I and Charles V go to war.

Portugal decides to own an Empire, and the Azores, Guinea, Madagascar, Sumatra, Malaysia and Bengal all fall to the Portuguese war machine. Not to be outdone, the Spaniards discover Florida, Peru and the West Indies. The first great religious war breaks out in the West in 1526, then another in 1567, a third ending in 1569.

The Turks take Cyprus in 1570 but lose it again in 1571 with the battle of Lepanto. French Protestants are massacred on Saint Bartholomew's Day in 1572, and the invincible Armada is soundly beaten in 1588.

Four years later, the Japanese invade Korea, but in 1603 the

Dutch land in Japan. Amazingly, the Poles have their moment of imperial glory in 1613 and take Moscow. The Thirty Years' War follows soon after. So does the Civil War in Britain, including a royal execution. The Turks return, and lay siege to Vienna. 1664 onwards sees a number of battles in western Europe including Blenheim. It all ends with a peace treaty in 1748. Eight years later, the Seven Years' War begins. Then there is the American War of Independence, and soon after the French Revolution creates another blood-bath, and the emergence of Napoleon Bonaparte means another twenty years of concentrated fighting.

After that episode, the scene returns to Arabia (1818), Russia v Turkey (1821), the USA v Mexico (1849), the Crimean War (1854–5), Spain v Peru and Chile (1858), American Civil War (1861), Prussia and Austria v Denmark (1864), Prussia v Austria (1866), Prussia v France (1870–1), Bulgaria v Turkey (1876), Russia v Turkey (1877), Bulgaria v Serbs (1885), China v Japan (1894), massacre of Armenians (same year), Boer War (1899–1902), Japan attacks Port Arthur (1904), Italy v Turkey (1911), Balkan States v Turkey (1912) and to the glorious war to end all wars, the Great War of 1914. Two years after its end, Greece and Turkey are at it again. War is banned at the Kellog Treaty in 1928. 1931: Japan invades China. 1935: Italy invades Ethiopia. 1936–38: the civil war in Spain. 1937: China and Japan again. 1939: the Second World War. As it ends, so another begins — this time in Vietnam (French involvement). 1947: bloody events in Palestine. Bloodier events in India. 1950–53: Korean War. 1955–62: War of Algerian Independence. 1956: the middle east again. Suez. 1959: Tibet — war between China and India. 1962–73: Vietnam (USA). 1963: Greeks and Turks do battle in Cyprus. 1965: Indo-Pakistan war. 1967: the Six Day War in the middle east. 1969-70 the Biafran conflict. 1969 to present day: the troubles in Northern Ireland. 1971–72: another Indo-Pakistan war. 1973: the Yom Kippur war in the middle east. 1975–76: war in the Lebanon. (Continues sporadically to the present day.) 1977: war between Somalia and Egypt. 1979: Vietnam v Cambodia. 1980: Russia invades Afghanistan (other interventions in Europe at various times from 1945 onwards). 1980 to present day: war between Iraq and Iran. 1983: Britain and Argentina do battle over the Falklands.

Appendix II
The My-Lai Massacre

The My-Lai massacre became a 'cause-célèbre' of the war in Vietnam, extensively reported by the world's press. A number of books have been written about it, including one by Seymour M. Hersh. Here are the facts:

On the morning of 10 March 1968, a company of American GIs were landed by helicopter near a Vietnamese hamlet which did not appear to contain any Vietcong fighting men. These GIs were under the command of Captain Medina, and their first section was under the orders of Lieutenant Calley. The people of this hamlet were mostly elderly, with some women and children, and they were eating at their front doors or inside their houses. They were bundled into the square, and with brutal and terrifying suddenness the killing started, to the sound of screams and moans of the dying. In a frenzy, soldiers were shooting at everything that moved, including animals, and emptying their guns into the huts, which were then set alight. According to Hersh, the soldiers did the job with pleasure: "The boys enjoyed it. When someone laughs and jokes about what they're doing, they have to be enjoying it. A GI said: 'Hey, I got me another one.' Another said: 'Chalk one up for me.'" It seems that Captain Medina and Lieutenant Calley paid for the rest, though certain witnesses saw them take an active part in the massacre, pushing people into a ditch, firing into the heaped bodies, finishing off the wounded, urging their men on. Hersh writes: "Herb Carter and Harry Stanley had shed their gear and were taking a short break at the CP (Command Post). Near them was a young Vietnamese boy, crying, with a bullet wound in his stomach. Stanley watched one of Captain Medina's three radio operators walk along a trail towards them. He . . . went up to Carter and said, 'let me see your pistol.' Carter gave it to him. The radio operator then stepped within two feet of the boy and shot him in the neck with the pistol. Blood gushed from the child's neck. He then tried to walk off, but he could only take two or three steps. Then he fell to the ground. He lay there and took four or five deep breaths and then he stopped breathing. The radio operator turned to Stanley and said, 'did you see how I shot that son-of-a-bitch?'"

By eleven o'clock the hamlet had ceased to exist. The ditch was full of bodies. Between 450 and 500 Vietnamese civilians had been massacred. On the American side, not one death and no wounded. Good clean work.

Appendix III
The 'Prayer to the Fuhrer'

The 'Prayer to the Führer' was published by the SS magazine *Das Schwurze Korps* to celebrate Hitler's fiftieth birthday on 20 April 1939:

"On this day I come before your presence. You are of supernatural greatness, your strength is without bounds. You are magnificent and sublime in your power, and in one person our father, our mother, our brother.

You are the Führer, always to be obeyed. You exist and you are among us. You are love and strength. You are freedom, for you have given us a sense of duty, making all work joyful, powerful and substantial. You have delivered our people from base and belittling tasks. The people fear you and in timid silence stay close to you, never leaving you. Your altar of love has been erected in the hearts of millions of people, to lead them towards the heavens in sunlight. On this day that we celebrate your birth, millions of hearts will beat faster and more strongly, and the sacred quality of your life among us will make this a day of supreme happiness for all Germans!"

Appendix IV
The Balila Catechism

"I believe in an eternal and intangible Rome, mother of my nation, enlightened and dominant heart of Europe's and the world's civilisation; and in Italy, her eldest and most glorious child, born of the wonder of God, from the virgin and fecund bosom of genius, of wisdom, of science, and the arts; suffered under a barbaric invader, was crucified, broken up and buried; descended into the ancients' tomb to take from their heart and soul, feelings and thoughts, and by them brought to life in the 19th century, lifted on high to her glory in 1918 and in 1922 through the triumph of Vittorio Veneto and the liberating victory of fascism; sits on the right hand of her mother Rome, intangible and eternal; from whence she will come to judge the living and the dead; I believe in the life-producing genius of Mussolini, and in the holy, brave and determined spirit of Italian people; in the Holy Father fascism, the communion of martyrs of the Alps, of the sea, the streets and squares with their partisans; the conversion of Italians who have lost their way and betrayed the cause, either through their own volition or by the grace of severe laws; the resurrection of the Roman Empire and its immortal and glorious life for ever — amen!"

(Balila Catechism taught to children of 8–12 in Italy during the thirties.)

Notes

1. Pierre-Joseph Proudhon: La Guerre et la Paix.
2. J. Novicow: Les Luttes entre les sociétés humaines.
3. R. von Jhering: The Spirit of Roman Law.
4. Napoleon 1: Works. "If I should be accused of liking war too much, then the historian will demonstrate that I was invariably the victim of aggression."
5. Col. von Rüstow: Kriegspol. und Kriegsgebrauch VIII.
6. Brandat: China Seas.
7. John Snail, Charlie Company, My Lai massacre.
8. Extract from an article by Daniel Lang in the New Yorker.
9. General Massu: la Bataille d'Alger.
10. Joseph de Maistre: Soirées de St. Petersbourg.
11. de Maistre: Considerations sur la France.
12. Deuteronomy.
13. Abbot-General, Dominican Order: Opus Tripartum.
14. St. Augustine.
15. Tavernier: Relation du Japon.
16. Extracts from Hierarchie Catholique et la guerre.
17. Joseph Rovan: le Catholicisme politique en Allemagne.
18. Abbé Lemerle: Tombés au champ d'honneur.
19. Redier-Hénocque: les Aumôniers militaires fançais.
20. Abbé Lemerle: idem.
21. Avro Manhattan: Der Vatikan und das XX Jahrhundert.
22. Joseph Proudhon: la Guerre et la Paix.
23. Adolf Lasson: Ib. Prob. Syst. des Rechtsphil.
24. Jean de Beuil, quoted in l'Armée à travers les âges.
25. Ellero: la Tirranida borghese.
26. Gumplovitz: la Lutte des races.
27. Chamberlain.
28. Doctrine of Action Française.
29. President Carter.
30. Karl Gothard Lamprecht.
31. Gioberti.
32. Official Soviet policy quoted in the Observer.
33. Motto of Japanese patriotic clubs.
34. Pierre Loti.
35. Léon Bloy.

36. Henri Lavedan, quoted in l'Intransigeant.
37. E. Meyr and D. Dobzhansky.
38. German S.S. Manual.
39. Michael Debré, quoted in Le Monde.
40. Jules Lemaître: l'Echo de Paris.
41. Marcel Sembat.
42. Albert Thomas
43. Abbé Lemerle: Tombés au champ d'honneur.
44. Lemaître.
45. Louis Legrand: l'Idée de patrie.
46. Bismarck.
47. Windham and Cook to Castlereagh.
48. The Economist.
49. L'Etoile belge.
50. Vacher de Lapouge, quoted by Lagorgette in Le Rôle de la guerre.
51. Joseph de Maistre.
52. René Quinton: Maximes de la guerre.
53. Quinton: idem.
54. Lépine: Hommes 40.
55. Herbert Spencer: Of Education.
56. Truppenführung.
57. Lépine: idem.
58. Quinton.
59. Lemerle: idem.
60. Louis Barthou, speech at the Sorbonne.
61. Maurice Genevoix: le Figaro littéraire.
62. Lavedan: idem.
63. Quinton: idem.
64. See Père de Sertillanges: le Bréviaire du combattant.
65. Liddell Hart: Thoughts on War.
66. US Admiral Mahan.

Bibliography

Adam (Paul), *La Cité prochaine, lettres de Malaisie*, Paris, Bibliothèque des auteurs modernes, 1908.

Adler (Moritz), "Enquête sur la guerre" from *l'Humanité nouvelle*, 1907.

Agathon (pseudonym of Henri Massis and Alfred de Tarde). *Les Jeunes Gens d'aujourd'hui*, Paris, Plon, 1913.

Akerhielm (pasteur Hans), *Le Glaive sous la Croix*, Genève, éditions Labor, 1942.

Alessandri (M.), *La Guerre et son droit*, Paris, éditions de Boccard, 1936.

Alexandre (Arsène), *Les Monuments français détruits par l'Allemagne*, Paris and Nancy, Berger-Levrault, 1918.

Allard (Paul), *La Guerre du mensonge, comment on nous a bourré le crâne*, Paris, éditions de France, 1940. — *Les Provocateurs à la guerre*, Paris, éditions de France, 1941. — *Ici, Londres!* Paris, éditions de France, 1942.

Alleg (Henri), *La Question*, Paris, les éditions de Minuit, 1958.

L'Ame française lettres de soldats morts pour la France, Montauban, Imprimerie coopérative Barrier et Co, 1922.

Andler (Charles), *Le Pangermanisme, ses plans d'expansion allemande dans le monde*, Paris, A. Colin, 1916.

Andraud (Henry), *Quand on fusillait les innocents*, Paris, Gallimard, 1935.

Arc (Pierre d'), pseudonym of Huot (abbé Pierre), *Le Bréviaire antiprussien...*, *Pensées françaises, Versets vengeurs, Fragments et souvenirs* Paris, P. Sevin, 1888.

Aron (Raymond), *Paix et guerre entre les nations*, Paris, Calmann-Lévy, 1962.

Arroy (Bezian), *Questions décidées sur la justice des armes des rois de France, sur les alliances avec les hérétiques ou infidèles et sur la conduite des gens de guerre*, Paris, G. Loison, 1634.

Aston (Major-general Sir George), *Secret Service, espionnage et contre-espionnage anglais pendant la guerre 14–18* French translation by Henry de Courtois, Paris, Payot, 1931.

L'Aumônerie militaire, 1870–1886, Paris, Imprimerie de Lutier, s.d.

Aziz (Phillippe), *Les Médecins de la mort*, Genève, Famot, 1974.

Barbier (abbé Paul), *Les Fruits de l'irréligion. L'irréligion et l'idée de patrie*, Paris, P. Lethielleux, s.d.

Barnaby (Dr C.F.), *Preventing the spread of nuclear weapons*, Souvenir Press, London, 1969.

Barth (Karl), *The Church and the war*, New York, Macmillan, 1944.

Bartsch (Rudolf Hans), *Das Deutsche Volk in Schwerer Zeit*, Berlin-Wien, Ullstein, 1916.

Basch (Victor), *Les Doctrines politiques des philosophes classiques de l'Allemagne, Leibniz, Kant, Fichte, Hegel*, Paris, Félix Alcan, 1927.

Bastiat (Frédéric), *Harmonies économiques*, Paris, Guillaumin, 1850.

Bataille (Georges), "La civilisation et la guerre", *Revue critique*, avril 1951.

Bazin (René), *Pages religieuses, temps de paix, temps de guerre*, Tours, Mame et Fils, 1915.

Béard (Dr Roger), *Les Expériences humaines dans les camps de concentration mazis pendant la Deuxième Guerre mondiale*, Nice, Imprimerie Barma, 1966.

Bellouard (abbé J.), *Un chant de consolation*, preface by Maurice Barrès, Niort, H. Boulord, 1916.

Bernadac (Christian), *Les Médecins maudits*, Paris, Presses Pocket, 1977.

Bernhardi (général Friedrich Adam Julius von), *Britain as Germany's vassal*, London, W. Dawson & Sons Ltd, 1914.

Bessières (Albert, S.J.), *L'Énvangile et la guerre*, Paris, Spes, 1939.

Bigeard (Marcel), *Pour une parcelle de gloire*, Paris, Plon, 1975.

Bigot (Charles), *Le Petit Français*, Primary School text book, Paris, E. Weill et G. Maurice, 1883.

Billig (Joseph), *Les Camps de concentration dans l'économie du Reich hitlérien*, Paris, les Presses Universitaires de France, 1973.

Billy (Charles), see "Lettres de Stalingrad".

Binet (René), *Théorie du racisme*, Paris, L'auteur, 1950.

Bismarck (comte Otto de), *Lettres de Bismarck à sa femme pendant la guerre de 1870*, Paris, J. Tallandier, 1903. — *The correspondence of William I & Bismarck*, London, Heinemann, 1903. — *Opinions et discours*, Paris, H. Gautier, s.d.

Blignières (Hervé de), *La Foi du centurion, le patriotisme principe d'action*, Paris, éditions du Fuseau, 1966.

Blondel (Georges), *La Guerre et le problème de la population*, Paris, P. Lethielleux, 1916.

Boasson (Marc), *Au soir d'un monde, lettres de guerre*, Paris, Plon, 1926.

Bodart (Gaston), *Losses of life in modern wars: Austria, Hungary, France*, Oxford, The Clarendon Press, 1916.

Bodin (Jean), *Les Six Livres de la République* (De Republica), Paris, J. Du Puys, 1576. En latin: *De Republica libri sex*, Paris, J. Du Puys, 1586.

Boguslawski (Albrecht von), *Der Krieg in seiner wahren Bedeutung für Staat und Volk*, Berlin, E.S. Mittler, 1892.

Bombardier X., *So this was war!* London, Hutchinson & Co. Ltd, s.d.

Bosc (Le père Robert, S.J.), *Évangile, violence et paix*, Paris, Le Centurion, 1975.

Bousquet (Raymond), *Force et stratégie nucléaire du monde moderne*, Paris/Limoges, Lavauzelle, 1974.

Bouthoul (Gaston), *Cent millions de morts*, Paris, Le Sagittaire, 1946. — *Huit mille traités de paix*, Paris, Julliard, 1948. — *Les Guerres, élément de polémologie*, Paris, Payot, 1951. — *Sauver la guerre*, Paris, Grasset, 1962.

Bouthoul (Gaston), et Carrère (René), *Le Défi de la guerre*, Paris, Presses Universitaires de France, 1976.

Brandat (Paul), pseudonym of Réveillère (admiral Paul-Émile Marie), *Mers de Chine*, Paris, Pichon et Co., 1872.

Brégeault (Pierre), *Heures mortes, poèmes de guerre*, Paris, Jouve, 1918.

Bristowe (William Syer), *A book of spiders*, New York, Penguin Books, 1947.

Brown (William), *War and peace*, London, Adam & Charles Black, 1939.

Brulé (Jean-Pierre), *L'Arsenal mondial*, Paris, Le Centurion, 1975.

Bruneau (général), *Vers héoïques, poèmes à lire et à dire*, Paris, Berger-Levrault, 1916, — *La gerbe d'or. Sonnets et poèmes*, Paris, Perrin et Co, 1924.

Cadoux (Gaston), *Nos pertes de guerre*, Paris, Berger-Levrault, 1926.

Cassan (Jacques de), La recherche des droicts du roy et de la couronne de France, sur les royaumes, duchez, comtés, villes et pays occupez par les princes étrangers, appartenant aux rois très chrétiens, etc. Paris, F. Pomeray, 1632.

Castier (Jules), *Les Heures guerrières*, Paris, 1920.

Cavaignac (Eugène), *Chronologie de l'histoire mondiale*, Paris, Payot, 1934.

Chamberlain (Houston Stewart), *Die Grundlagen des neunzehnten Jahrhunderts* (Les fondements du XIXe siècle), München, F. Bruckmann, 1899.

Champion (Félix), *Ne pereant, Rimes et souvenirs illustrés, 1914-1918*, Vire, Imprimerie de J. Beaufils, 1930.

Chao-Kung, *La guerre peut-elle être abolie? Le problème de la vie*, Paris, Parisis Edition, 1934.

Chardonnet (Jean), *Les Conséquences économiques de la guerre 1939-1945*, Paris, Hachette, 1947.

Charpentier (Armand), *La Guerre et la patrie*, Paris, André Delpeuch, 1926.

Chasles (Madeleine), *La Guerre et la Bible* Paris, Je sers, 1940.

Chauvin (Rémy), *Les Sociétés animales, de l'abeille au gorille*, Paris, Plon, 1963. — *Techniques de combat chez les animaux*, Paris, Hachette, 1965. — *Le Monde des fourmis*, Paris, Plon, 1969.

Chayer (Henri), *Les Crimes des Boches*, Paris, 1917.

Choppin (capitaine Henri), *Patrie et guerre*, Paris, Berger-Levrault, 1915.

Chossat (Marcel S.J.), *La Guerre et la paix d'après le droit naturel chrétien*, Paris, Bloud et Gay, 1918.

Cianfarra (Camille), *La Guerre et le Vatican (39-45)*, Paris, Le Portalan, 1947.

Cinquante poèmes à dire, Paris, Berger-Levrault, 1915.

Clarke (Robin), *La Course à la mort ou la technocratie de la guerre* French translation by Georges Renard, Paris, Le Seuil, 1972. — *La Guerre biologique est-elle pour demain?*, Paris, Fayard, 1972.

Claude (Henri), *De la crise économique à la guerre mondiale*, Paris, édition O.C.I.A., 1945.

Clausewitz (Carl von), *De la guerre*, Paris, les Éditions de Minuit, 1955.

Clemenceau (Georges), *Grandeurs et misères d'une victoire*, Paris, Plon, 1930. — *Discours de guerre*, Paris, Plon, 1934.

Cloquié (Mme H.), *Les Soldats de France de 1914-1915*, Paris, Maloine, 1915.

Coates (John Rider), *War, what does the Bible say?* London, Sheldon Press, 1940.

Collignon (Dr René), *Résumé des travaux scientifiques de M. le docteur René Collignon*, Cherbourg, Imprimerie de E. Le Maout, 1900

Combris (Andrée), *La philosophie des races du comte de Gobineau et sa portée actuelle* (thèse), Paris, Alcan, 1937.

Consentini (Francesco), "Le militarisme de l'avenir", *Revue internationale sociale*, 1899.

Constantin (capitaine André), *Le Rôle sociologique de la guerre et le sentiment national, suivi de La Guerre, moyen de sélection collective*, traduit de l'ouvrage du Dr F. Steinmetz, *Der Krieg als sociologisches Problem*, paru à Amsterdam chez W. Wersluys en 1899, Paris, Félix Alcan, 1907. — *Guerre et démographie*, Lyon, J. Desvignes et ses fils, 1929.

Costel (Paul), *Chants de la guerre, poèmes*, Paris, E. Figuière, 1915.

Cotereau (Jean), *L'Église a-t-elle collaboré?* Paris, éditions de l'Idée libre, 1946.

Coüannier (André Henry), *Légitimité de la guerre aérienne*, Paris, Per Orbem, 1925.

Coubard (Jacques), *La Guerre des six jours*, Paris, éditions sociales, 1973.

Coubé (Le R.P. Stephen, S.J.), *Sainte Thérèse de l'Enfant Jésus et la crise du temps présent*, Paris, Flammarion, 1936. — *L'âme du soldat*, Paris, Victor Retaux, 1899.

Cousin (Victor), Cours de l'histoire de la philosophie, Paris, Pichon et Didier, 1828.

Crozals (Jacques-Marie de), *Histoire de la civilisation depuis les temps antiques jusqu'à Charlemagne*, Paris, C. Delagrave, 1885.

Cru (Jean Norton), *Témoins*, Paris, les Étincelles, 1929.

Daguet (Hippolyte), *Sonnets sur la guerre*, Imprimerie de Monnoyer, 1915.

Daniel (Joseph), "Guerre et cinéma. Grandes illusions et petits soldats", 1895–1971, Paris, *Cahiers de la Fondation nationale des Sciences politiques*, Armand Colin, 1972.

Dartein (abbé) de) et Decout (le Père Alexis, S.J.), *Manuel de l'aumônerie militaire de la marine et du prêtre mobilisé*, Paris, éditions Alsatia, 1939.

Darwin (Charles Robert), *De l'origine des espèces, ou des lois du progrès chez les êtres organisés* traduit en français par Mlle Clémence Auguste Royer, Paris, Guillaumin, 1862. — *La Descendance de l'homme et la sélection naturelle*, traduit de l'anglais par J.-J. Moulinié, Paris, C. Reinwald, 1872.

Delarue (Jacques), *Histoire de la Gestapo*, Paris, Fayard, 1962.

Delarue-Mardrus (Lucie), see *Cinquante poèmes à dire*.

Delaveau (Pierre), *Plantes agressives et poisons végétaux*, Paris, Bordas, 1974.

Delorme (Jean), *Chronologie des civilisations*, Paris, Presses Universitaires de France, 1949.

Delsol (Ferdinand), *Chants de la Grande Guerre, poèmes*, Paris, Éditions et Publications contemporaines, Pierre Bossuet, 1928.

Demartial (Georges), *Le Mythe des guerres de légitime défense*, Paris, Marcel Rivière, 1931.

Der Deutsche Krieg in Feldpostbriefen, München, G. Müller, 1915.

Derrecagaix (général Victor Bernard), *La Guerre moderne*, Paris, L. Baudouin, 1885.

Destrains (Jean), *La France victorieuse, poème national*, préface d'Émile Faguet, Paris, A. Lemerre, 1915.

Devaldès (Manuel), *Croître et multiplier, c'est la guerre*, Paris, G. Mignolet et Storz, 1933. — *La Guerre dans l'acte sexuel*, Châtillon-sous-Bagneaux, Publication du pacifisme scientifique, 1936.

Diedisheim (Jean), *Les Patries — vers une mutation du mode de penser*, Neufchâtel, éditions de la Baconnière, 1967.

Dragomirof (général), *La Guerre est un mal inévitable*, Paris, Lavauzelle, 1897.

Dubarle (capitaine Robert), *Lettres de guerre*, Paris, Perrin, 1918.

Dubois (Dr. Raphaël), *Les Origines naturelles de la guerre, influences cosmiques et théorie anticinétique, la paix par la science*, Lyon, H. Georg, 1916.

Duclos (Paul), *Le Vatican et la Deuxième Guerre mondiale*, Paris, A. Pedone, 1955.

Ducrocq (Albert), *Les Armes de demain*, Paris, Berger-Levrault, 1948.

Duhelly (Jacques), *Philosophie de la guerre*, Paris, Félix Alcan, 1921.

Dumont (Gérard-Fraçois), avec la collaboration de Chaunu (Pierre),

Legrand (Jean), Sauvy (Alfred), *La France ridée*, Le Livre de Poche, Paris, Librairie générale française, 1979.

Dumont (René), *L'Utopie ou la mort!*, Paris, Le Seuil, 1973.

Dupuy (Pierre), *Traité touchant les droits du Roy très chrétien sur plusieurs estats et seigneureries possédées par divers princes voisins,* Paris, 1655.

Dvorjecki (Dr Marc), *La Stérilisation criminelle nazie dans les camps de concentration*, Paris, Imprimerie Abécé, 1957.

Ehrlich (Paul), *La Bombe P.*, Paris, éditions J'ai lu, 1973.

Ellero (Pietro), *La Tirranide borghese*, Bologne, tip. Fava e Garagnani, 1879.

Engelbrecht (H.C.) et Hanighen (F.C.), *Marchands de mort* (The merchants of death), Paris, Flammarion, 1934.

Ermenonville, pseudonym of Dupin (Gustave), *Le Collier de Bellone* Paris, Société mutuelle d'édition, 1924.

Estoc (Martial d'), pseudonym of Dumont (Auguste), *Le Génie de la guerre. Le développement, les erreurs et la logique de la guerre*, Paris, A. Dumont, 1892.

Fawzia Al-Rubaci, *Terrorism and concentration camps in Israel*, Baghdad, Taqquadum Press, 1970.

Feytaud (Jean de), *Le Peuple des termites*, Paris, Presses Universitaires de France, 1966.

Filloux (Jean-Claude), *Psychologie des animaux*, Paris, Presses Universitaires de France, 1965.

Foch (general, then marshal), *Les Principes de la guerre*, Paris, Berger-Levrault, 1903.

Folliet (Joseph), *Pour comprendre les prisonniers. (De la captivité comme expérience humaine)*, Paris, Le Seuil, 1943.

Fontette (François de), *Le Racisme*, collection "Que sais-je?", Paris, Presses Universitaires de France, 1975.

Forel (Dr Auguste), *Les Fourmis de la Suisse*, La Chaux-de-Fonds, 1920 — *Homme et fourmi*, Lausanne, 1923.

Fouillée (Alfred), *Esquisse psychologique des peuples européens*, Paris, Félix Alcan, 1903.

Frédéric II le Grand, roi de Prusse, *Anti-Machiavel ou Essai de critique sur "Le Prince" de Machiavel, La Haye, P. Paupie, 1740.*

Freud (Sigmund), Trois Essais sur la théorie de la sexualité, traduits de l'allemand par le docteur B. Reverchon, Paris, Gallimard, 1949.

Galbraith (J.K.), see *la Paix indésirable?*

Galipaux, *Petits Vers sur de grands mots*, Paris, s.d.

Garaude (abbé François), *La guerre, considérée au point de vue philosophique, social et religieux*, Paris, A. Bray, 1864.

Gaulle (Charles de), *Le Fil de l'épée*, Paris, Berger-Levrault, 1932.

Genevoix (Maurice), *Au seuil des guitounes*, Paris, Flammarion, 1918. —

Les Éparges, Paris, Flammarion, 1923.

Gérin (René), *Les Causes psychologiques des guerres*, Paris, Ligue inter-nationale des Combattants de la Paix, 1935.

Ghilini (Hector), *La Troisième Guerre mondiale durera six heures*, Paris, R. Seban, 1950.

Gillespie (Robert Dick), *Psychological effects of war on citizen and soldier*, London, Chapman & Hall, 1942.

Giordani (Iginio), *La Révolution de la Croix*, Paris, Alsatia, 1938.

Giovanniti (Len) et Fred (Freed), *Histoire secrète d'Hiroshima* (The decision to drop the bomb). French translation by Pierre Francart, Paris, Plon, 1966.

Giran (abbé Étienne), *L'Évangile et la guerre*, Carrières-sous-Poissy, "La Cause", 1939.

Giraudoux (Jean), *La Folle de Chaillot*, Paris, Grasset, 1948.

Glucksman (André), *Le Discours de la guerre*, collection "10/18", Paris, éditions de l'Herne, 1974.

Gobineau (comte Joseph Arthur de), *Essai sur l'inégalité des races humaines*, 2ᵉ édition, Paris, Firmin-Didot, 1884.

Gohier (Degoulet Urbain, dit), *L'Armée contre la nation*, Paris, éditions de la "Revue Blanche", 1898.

Goodheart (A.L.), *What acts of war are justifiable*, Oxford, Clarendon Press, 1941.

Grassé (P.), *Précis de zoologie*, Paris, Masson, 1961.

Grosclaude (Pierre), *Alfred Rosenberg et le "Mythe du XXᵉ siècle"*, Paris, F. Sorlot, 1938.

Grotius (Hugo de Groot, dit), *Le Droit de la guerre et de la paix*. Traduit du latin par M. de Courtin, Paris, A. Seneuze, 1687.

Guerber (André), *Himmler et ses crimes*, Paris, les Documents nuit et jour, Fournier, 1946.

Guillaume II (Les discours de Guillaume II pendant la guerre), Paris, Bossard, 1918.

Guillaumin (Colette), *L'Idéologie raciste — genèse et langage actuel*, Paris, La Haye, Mouton, 1972.

Guitton (Jean), *Journal de captivité 1942–1943. Extraits*, Paris, Aubier, 1943.

Gumplovicz (Ludwick), *La Lutte des races, recherches sociologiques*. Translation by Charles Baye. Paris, Guillaumin, 1893.

Guyau (Jean-Marie), *Esquisse d'une morale sans obligation ni sanction*, Paris, Félix Alcan, 1885.

Hackett (general Sir John), *The third world war, August 1985*. London, Sidgwick & Jackson, 1978.

Hart (captain Basil Henry Liddell), *Thoughts on war*, London, Faber & Faber, 1944.

Haskins (Caryl Parker), *Of Ants and men*, London, Allen & Unwin, 1945.

Heering (G.J.), *Dieu et César. La carence des Églises devant le problème de la guerre*. Translated by H. Rochot, Paris, Société commerciale d'édition et de librairie. 1933.

Henches (Jules-Émile), *Lettres de guerre*, Cahors, 1917.

A l'école de la guerre, lettres d'un artilleur, août 1914–octobre 1916, Paris, Hachette, 1918.

Henry (colonel R.), *L'Esprit de la guerre moderne, d'après les grands capitaines et les philosophes*, Paris, Berger-Levrault, 1894.

Hersch (professeur L.), *Effets démographiques de la guerre moderne* Paris, 1934.

Hersh (Seymour M.), *My Lai Massacre*. Translated by Georges Magnane, Paris, Gallimard, 1970.

Hersey (John), *Hiroshima*, London, Penguin Books, 1946.

Heysman (colonel Piaton Aleksandrovitch de), *La Guerre, son importance dans la vie du peuple et de l'État* Translation by capitaine Niessel, Paris, H. Charles Lavauzelle 1898.

La hiérarchie catholique et la guerre, Paris, Bonne Presse, 1940.

Histoires de fin du monde, présentées par Jacques Goimard, Demetre Iokimidis et Gérard Klein, Le Livre de Poche, Paris, Librairie général française, 1974.

Hitler (Adolf), *Mein Kampf* (Mon Combat). Translation by J. Gaudefroy-Demombynes et A. Calmettes, Paris, Nouvelles Éditions latines, s.d.

Hoess (Rudolf Franz Ferdinand), *Le Commandant d'Auschwitz parle*. Translation by Constantin de Grunwald. Paris, Julliard, 1959.

Hofer (Walther), *Le National-Socialisme par les textes*. Translation by G. et L. Marcou, Paris, Plon, 1962.

Hornaday (William Temple), *The minds and manners of wild animals* New York and London, C. Scribner's Sons, 1922.

Horvath (Odon de), *Soldat du Reich*. Translation by Armand Pierhal, Paris, Plon, 1940.

Hubert (René), *Les Interprétations de la guerre*, Paris, Flammarion, 1919.

Hueber (Édouard), *Du rôle de l'armée dans l'État et des principes de l'institution militaire*, Paris, Berger-Levrault, 1872.

Huxley (Aldous Leonard), *Ends & Means. An enquiry into the nature of ideals and into the methods employed for their realization*, London, Chatto & Windus, 1937.

Ibarrola (Jésus), *Les Incidence des deux conflits mondiaux sur l'évolution démographique française*, Paris, Dalloz, 1964.

Imms (Augustus Daniel), *Social behaviour in insects*, London, Methuen & Co., 1931.

Iung (général Théodore), *La Guerre et la société*, Paris, Berger-Levrault, 1889.

Jähns (Max), *Ueber Krieg, Frieden und Kultur, eine Umschau*, Berlin, allgemeiner Verein für deutsche Litteratur, 1893.

Jhering ou Ihering (Rudolf von), *Le Combat pour le droit*. Translation by Alexandre-François Meydieu, Vienne, G.J. Manz, 1875. — *L'Ésprit du droit romain dans les diverses phases de son développement*. Translation by O. de Meulenacre, Paris, A. Maresq aîné, 1880.

Jomini (général Antoine-Henry de), *Précis de l'art de la guerre*, Paris, Anselin, 1838.

Journées Universitaires (34ᵉ), "Le patriotisme", Paris, 1957.

Juganaru, *L'Apologie de la guerre dans la philosophie contemporaine*, Paris, Félix Alcan, 1933.

Jünger (Ernst), *La Guerre, notre mère*, Paris, Albin Michel, 1934.

Kahn (Herman), *On Thermonuclear war*, Princeton, Princeton University Press, 1961.

Kant (Emmanuel), *Critique du jugement*, suivie des *Observations sur le sentiment du beau et du sublime*. Translation by J. Barni. Paris, Lagrange, 1846.

Kapeliouk (Amnou), *Israël, la fin des mythes*, Paris, Albin Michel, 1975.

Kellog (Vernon Lyman), *Military selection & race deterioration*, Oxford, The Clarendon Press, 1916.

Keramane (Hafid), *La Pacification*, Lausanne, La Cité, 1960.

Kessel (P.) et Pirelli (G.), *Le Peuple algérien et la guerre* (Lettres et témoignages d'Algériens), Paris, Maspero, 1963.

Kissinger (Henry A.), *Le Chemin de la paix*. Translation by Henri Drevet, Paris, le Club français du Livre, 1973.

Klein (Gérard), voir *Histoires de fin du monde*.

Knox (Ronald), *God and the Atom*, London, Sheed & Ward, 1945.

La Barre Duparcq (colonel Édouard), *Commentaires sur le traité "De la guerre" de Clausewitz*, Paris, J. Corréard, 1853.

La Brière (le Père Yves de, S.J.), *Les Droits et devoirs des belligérants d'après la morale chrétienne*, Paris, Alsatia, 1940. — *Le Droit de juste guerre. Tradition théologique. Adaptations contemporaines*, Paris, Pedone, 1938.

Lacaze-Duthiers (Gérard de), *La Torture à travers les âges*, Herblay, éditions de l'Idée libre, 1956.

Lacombe (Jean-Marie), *Amours et trophées*, Paris, édition de la Librairie montmartoise, 1916.

Lacombe (Paul), *La Guerre et l'homme*, Paris, G. Bellais, 1900.

Lacordaire (R.P. Henri-Dominique), *Éloge funèbre du général Drouot (25 mai 1847)*, Paris, Sagnier et Bray, 1847.

La Fayette (général Marie-Joseph-Paul-Roch-Yves-Gilbert du Mottier, Marquis de), *Adresse à l'armée française (1ᵉʳ mai 1792)*, Rouen, Le Héribel, s.d.

Lagneau (Dr Gustave), *Conséquences démographiques qu'ont eues pour la France les guerres depuis un siècle*, Orléans, Imprimerie de P. Giraudot, 1892.

Lagorgette (Jean), *Le Rôle de la guerre, étude de sociologie générale*, Paris, V. Giard et E. Brière, Libraires-Éditeurs, 1906.

Lammasch, *Voelkermord oder Voelkerbund*, La Haye, 1920.

Lane (Mark), *Les Soldats américains accusent*, Les Cahiers libres 238-239, Paris, Maspero, 1972.

Larroque (Patrice), *De la guerre et des armées permanentes*, Paris, Guillaumin, 1856.

Lartéguy (Jean), *Ces voix qui nous viennent de la mer*. Lettres recueillies, adaptées et présentées par Jean Lartéguy, translated in collaboration with Suzanne Audray et Ko Iwasé, Paris, Gallimard, 1954.

Lasson (Adolf), *Princip und Zukunft des Völkerrechts*, Berlin, G. Hertz, 1871.

Latzko (Andréas), *Le Général Lafayette*. Translated by Alexandre Vialatte, Paris, Grasset, 1935.

Laurent (François), *Études sur l'histore de l'humanité*, Gand, H. Hoste; Paris, A. Durand, 1855-1870 (18 volumes).

Lauret (Jean-Claude) et Lasierra (Raymond), *La Torture et les pouvoirs*, Paris, Balland, 1973.

Le Bon (Dr Gustave), *Les Lois psychologiques de l'évolution des peuples*, Paris, Félix Alcan, 1894. — *Premières Conséquences de la guerre 14-18. Transformation mentale des peuples*. Paris, Flammarion, 1917.

Lebreton (Jules), *Pensées chrétiennes sur la guerre*, Paris, Gabriel Beauchesne, 1916.

Le Dantec (Félix), *L'Égoïsme, seule base de toute société, étude des déformations résultant de la vie en commun*, Paris, Flammarion, 1911. — *La Lutte universelle*, Paris, Flammarion, 1906.

Legrand (Louis-Désiré), *L'Idée de patrie*, Paris, Hachette, 1897.

Lemerle (Abbé), *Tombés au champ d'honneur*, Paris, P. Lethielleux, 1925.

Lépine (Jean), *Hommes 40, chevaux (en long) 8,* Paris, éditions René Hilsum & Co (Au sans Pareil), 1933.

Lestoquoy (Mgr Jean), *Histoire du patriotisme en France, des origines à nos jours*, Paris, Albin Michel, 1968.

Letourneau (Charles), *La Guerre dans les diverses races humaines*, Paris, L. Bataille, 1895.

Letters from the front, selected and published by John Laffin, London, J.M. Dent & Sons Ltd, 1973.

Lettres de Stalingrad, Translated by Charles Billy. Paris, Buchet-Chastel, 1974.

Lettres d'étudiants allemands tués à la guerre (1914-1918), chosen by professeur Ph. Witkop and translated by E. Herrmann. Préface et post-scriptum de Paul Desjardins. Les documents bleus. Notre temps, no 26, Paris, Gallimard, 1932.

Levasseur (G.), *L'Église et la guerre*, Paris, Bureau d'édition, 1933.

Lévi-Strauss (Claude), *Race. Histoire*, Paris, Gonthier, 1967.

Lewal (général), *La Chimère du désarmement*, Paris, L. Baudouin, 1897.

Lewinsohn (Richard), *Les Profits de guerre à travers les siècles*, Paris, Payot, 1935.

Le Wita (Henri), *Autour de la guerre chimique; comment éviter ce fléau*, Paris, J. Tallandier, 1928.

Lombroso (Cesare), *L'Homme, criminel-né, fou moral, épileptique, étude anthropologique et médico-Légale*. Paris, Félix Alcan, 1887. — *Le Crime, causes et remèdes*, Paris, Schleicher frères, 1899.

Lorenz (Konrad), *L'Agression, une histoire naturelle du mal*. Translated by Vilma Fritsh, Paris, Flammarion, 1968.

Lorson (Pierre, S.J.), *Un chrétien peut-il être objecteur de conscience?* Paris, Le Seuil, 1950.

Lorulot (André), *Barbarie allemande et barbarie universelle: le livre rouge des atrocités mondiales*, Conflans-Sainte-Honorine, éditions de "l'Idée libre", 1921. — *L'Église et la guerre*, Paris, éditions de "l'Idée libre", 1932.

Louveaux (Jean), *Plantes carnivores et végétaux hostiles*, Paris, Hachette, 1965.

Ludendorf (général), *La Guerre totale*, Paris, Flammarion, 1936.

Mabille (Paul), *La Guerre, ses lois, son influence civilisatrice, sa perpétuité*, Paris, A. Fourneau, 1884.

Mailles (chanoine Auguste), *Pour Dieu, pour la France. Avant, pendant la guerre*, Paris, Jouve, 1916.

Maistre (Comte Joseph de), *Considérations sur la France*, Lyon, E. Vitte, 1924. (1er Édition, Londres, 1797). — *Les Soirées de Saint-Pétersbourg, ou entretiens sur le gouvernement de la Providence, suivis d'un traité sur les sacrifices*, Paris, Librairie grecque, latine et française, 1821.

Mangenot (chanoine Eugène), *Dictionnaire de théologie catholique, contenant l'exposé des doctrines de la théologie catholique, leurs preuves et leur histoire*, Paris, 1903-1927.

Manhattan (Avro), *The catholic Church against the 20th century*, London, Watts & Co, 1947.

Mao Tsé-Toung. Écrits choisis en trois volumes. Traduction et notes de l'édition officielle de Pékin, Paris, Maspero, 1967.

Marcaux (Jean), *Honneur et patrie! Des mots à la réalité*, Paris, éditions de la Pensée nouvelle, 1950.

Marthold (Jules de), *Chant de haine, réponse à Berlin*, Paris, Librairie anglo-française, 1915.

Martin De Condé (Henry Hector), *Chants de guerre*, Billancourt, Imprimerie de A. Mercier, 1907. — *Poésies guerrières*, Paris, Librairie littéraire, 1915.

Masson (Pierre Maurice), *Lettres de guerre, août 1914–avril 1916*, Paris, Hachette, 1917.

Massu (général Jacques), *La Vraie Bataille d'Alger*, Paris, Plon, 1971.

Matter (Florent), *Diplomatie et duplicité prussiennes. Les vrais criminels*. Nancy, Paris, Strasbourg, Berger-Levrault, 1926.

Mc Innis, *The war*, Oxford University Press, London, 1940.

Méjasson (Joseph), *Ce que tout soldat français doit savoir d'allemand*, Lyon, E. Vitte, 1915.

Mellor (Alec), *La Torture, son histoire, son abolition, sa réapparition au XXe siècle*, Paris, les Horizons littéraires, 1949.

Menkès (Dr G.), Hermann (Dr R.), et Miège (Dr A.), *Cobayes humains*, Paris, Éditions des trois collines, 1946.

Merlaud (André), *Le Christ dans la tranchée, mai–juin 1940*, Paris, Bonne Presse, 1944.

Meuley (abbé Achille), *Les Boches, odes guerrières 1914–1915*, Sceaux, Imprimerie de Charaire, 1915.

Meynier (A), *Une erreur historique. Les morts de la Grand Armée et des armées ennemies*, Paris, Presses Universitaires de France, 1930

Mezières (Louis), *De la polémomanie ou folie de la guerre dans l'Europe actuelle*, Paris, H. Bellaire, 1872.

Michelson (A.), *Le Financement de la guerre et les problèmes de la reconstruction*, Paris, R. Pichon et R. Durand-Auzias, 1945.

Mitchell (Peter Chalmers), *Le Darwinisme et la guerre*, Paris, Alcan, 1916.

Mitton (Fernand), *Tortures et supplices à travers les âges*, Paris, H. Daragon, 1908.

Moloy (P.J. de), *François-Joseph I et Gullaume II. Le front!* Saïgon, Imprimerie saïgonnaise, 1915.

Montaigne (lieutenant-colonel Jean-Baptiste), *Vaincre. Esquisse d'une doctrine de la guerre basée sur la connaissance de l'homme et sur la morale*, Paris, Berger-Levrault, 1913.

Moreau-Vauthier, *Vivent les poilus!* Paris, Jouve, s.d.

Mumford (Lewis), *Technique et civilisation*. Translated by Denise Moutonnier, Paris, Le Seuil, 1976.

Naquet (Alfred), *L'Humanité et la patrie*, P.V. Stock, 1901.

Naudeau (Ludovic), *La Guerre et la paix. Avec l'opinion des plus illustres penseurs et hommes d'État français*, Paris, Flammarion, 1926.

Netter (rabbin Nathan), *La Souffrance, quelle divine méconnue!* Metz, Imprimerie P. Event, 1924.

Newman (Keith Odo), *Mind, sex and war. Blackouts, fear of air raids, propaganda*, Oxford, Pelagos Press, 1941.

Nietzsche (Frederic), *Ainsi parlait Zarathoustra*, Paris, Mercure de France, 1898.

Novalis (Friedrich von Hardenberg, dit), *Henri d'Ofterdingen*. Translated and adapted by Georges Polti et Paul Morisse, Paris, Société du "Mercure de France", 1908.

Novicow (J.), *La Guerre et ses prétendus bienfaits*, Paris, A. Colin, 1894. — *Les Luttes entre les sociétés humaines et leurs phases successives*, Paris, Félix Alcan, 1893.

Olliver (R.P. François-Marie-Joseph), *La Guerre*, Sermon prononcé en l'église de la Madeleine à Paris, le 17 avril 1896 au service des Français morts à Madagascar, Paris, P. Lethielleux, s.d.

Orwell (George), *Nineteen eighty four*, A novel. London, Penguin Books, 1954.

La paix indésirable, "Report from iron mountain on the possibility and desirability of peace" translated by Jean Bloch-Michel, preface by J.K. Galbraith, Paris, Calmann-Lévy, 1968.

Panici (Pére, S.J.), *La France en guerre, nos devoirs de chrétiens*, Paris, La Bonne Presse, 1939.

Paris (Edmond), *Le Vatican contre la France*, Paris, éditions Fischbacker, 1957. — *Le Vatican contre l'Europe*, Paris, éditions Fischbacker, 1959.

Parrot (Louis), *L'Intelligence en guerre*, Paris, la Jeune Parque, 1945.

Paterni (Joseph), *Accents d'épopée! 1914-1917*, Nice, Imprimerie de J. Gasparini, 1917.

Payen (chanoine Joseph Eugène), *L'Ame du poilu. Journal de route d'un aumônier militaire du 7ᵉ Corps, pendant la Grande Guerre 1914-1918*, Besançon, Imprimerie de Jacques et Demontrond, 1924.

Pergaud (Louis), *Mélanges*, Paris, Mercure de France, 1938.

Peyronnard (J.), Université de Montpellier, Faculté de droit. *Des causes de la guerre*. Thèse pour le doctorat ès-sciences politiques et économiques, Montpellier, Imprimerie de Delord-Boehm et Martial, 1901.

Philonenko (Alexis), *Essai sur la philosophie de la guerre*, Paris, Vrin, 1976.

Pichon (Charles), *Histoire du Vatican,* Paris, Société d'éditions françaises et internationales, 1946.

Pingaud (Albert), *La Guerre vue par les combattants allemands*, Paris, Perrin, 1918.

Poliakof (Léon), *Bréviaire de la haine; le IIIᵉ Reich et les Juifs*, Paris Le Livre de Poche, 1974. — *Le Mythe aryen, essai sur les sources du racisme et des nationalismes*, Paris, Calmann-Lévy, 1971.

"Politique germanophile du Vatican pendant la guerre de 1914", la Brochure républicaine, no 2, Paris, 1924.

Poncet (Alice), *Fleur d'héroïsme, le poème national de la Grande Guerre, chanté par le coq gaulois et l'alouette française*, Lamalou-les-Bains (Hérault), édition de la Revue du Languedoc et des jeux floraux, 1916.

Ponsonby (Arthur), *Falsehood in war-time, an amazing collection of carefully documented lies circulated in Great Britain, France, Germany, Italy, America during the great war*, London, Allen & Unwin, 1928.

Prévost-Paradol (Lucien Anatole), *Essais de politique et de littérature*, Paris, Michel-Lévy frères, 1859.

Pro-Patria (août–septembre 1914), "Guerz", Chants guerriers du druide ex-officier d'état-major de la garde nationale en 1970. Paris,

Imprimerie de C. Piton, 1914.

Proudhon (Pierre-Joseph), *La Guerre et la paix, recherches sur le principe et la constitution du droit des gens*, Paris, Michel-Lévy frères, 1861.

Pujo (Maurice), *La Guerre et l'homme*, Paris, Flammarion, 1932.

Pulsford (Edward J.), *Should Christians fight? An answer based on the Christian Sacred Scripture, in the light of the teaching of Emmanuel Swedenborg*, London, New Church Missionary and Tract Society, 1940.

Queval (Jean), *Première Page, cinquième colonne*, Paris, Fayard, 1945.

Quinton (René), *Maximes sur la guerre*, Paris, Grasset, 1930.

Le Racisme et la Science, Unesco, 1960, Paris, nouvelle édition, 1973.

Rasteil (Maxim Rastoil, dit), *L'Épopée théâtrale 1914-1918*, Paris, Société mutuelle d'édition, 1924.

Rauschning (Hermann), *Hitler m'a dit. Confidences du Führer sur son plan de conquête du monde*. Translated by Albert Lehman. Paris, Coopération, 1939.

Reboux (Paul), *Les Drapeaux*, roman, Paris, Flammarion, 1921.

Redelsperger (Jacques), *Au frisson des drapeaux*, poèmes de guerre, Paris, Ligue "Souvenez-nous", s.d.

Redier (Antoine) et Henocque (abbé G.), *Les Aumôniers militaires français*, Paris, Flammarion, 1940.

Régnier (Henri de), *Poésies*, Paris, Mercure de France, 1918.

Reichenau (général von), *Einfluss der Kultur auf Krieg und Kriegsrüstung*, Berlin, E.S. Mittler und sohn, 1897.

Reiner (Silvain), *Et la terre sera pure . . .*, Paris, Fayard, 1969.

Remarque (Erich Maria), *All Quiet on the Western Front, A l'Ouest rien de nouveau*, Paris, Stock, 1929.

Remy, *Catéchisme de la patrie*, Paris, éditions France-Empire, s.d.

Renan (Ernest), *La Réforme intellectuelle et morale*, Paris, Michel-Lévy frères, 1871.

Reppelin (Léon), *Sous les ailes de la mort. Poèmes du front 14-17*, Montauban, Imprimeries de Barrier, 1918.

Réveillaud (Eugène), *La Lyre d'airain du vieux barde*, poèmes patriotiques et stances sur les peuples engagés dans la guerre mondiale, Paris, Berger-Levrault, 1918.

Reves (Emery), *Anatomie de la paix*, Paris, éditions Tallendier, 1946.

Rey (Abel), *Le Retour éternel et la philosophie de la physique*, Paris, Flammarion, 1927.

Rey (Benoît), *Les Égorgeurs*, Paris, les Éditions de Minuit, 1961.

Richet (Charles), *La Paix et la guerre*, Paris, 8 rue de la Sorbonne, 1905.

Rivet (Gustave), *L'Épopée, poème*, Paris, E. Figuière, 1918.

Robson (Walter), *Letters from a soldier*, London, Faber & Faber, 1960.

Roessler (Constantin), *System der Staatslehre*, Leipzig, Falcke und Roessler, 1857.

Romocki (S.J. von), *Geschichte des Explosivstoffe* (Histoire des matières explosives) Berlin, R. Oppenheim (Gustav Schmidt), 1895–1896.

Roulx (Didier de), *Les Sonnets de la victoire*, précédés d'un sonnet-dédicace de Henri de Régnier, Paris, éditions de la Jeune École, 1916.

Roux (René), *Le Vatican et la Deuxième Guerre mondiale*, Paris, A. Pedone, 1956.

Rovan (Joseph), *Le Catholicisme politique en Allemagne*, Paris, Le Seuil, 1956.

Russell (Lord Bertrand), *Justice in war-time*, London, Allen & Unwin, 1924.

Rustow (Friedrich Wilhelm), *Kriegspolitik und Kriegsgebrauch, Studien und Betrachtungen*, Zurich, F. Schulthess, 1876.

Ruyssen (Théodore), *De la guerre au droit, étude de philosophie sociale*, Paris, Félix Alcan, 1920.

Sageret (Jules), *Philosophie de la guerre et de la paix*, Paris, Félix Alcan, 1919.

Salvioli (Giuseppe), *Le Concept de la guerre juste d'après les écrivains antérieurs à Grotius*, traduit de l'Italien, Paris, Bossard, 1918.

Sarrazin (Louis), *Les Vengeresses*, Toulouse, 1915.

Sauvy (Alfred, *La Population, sa mesure, ses mouvements, ses lois, 13ᵉ éditions mise à jour, Paris collection "Que sais-je", Presses Universitaires de France, 1979. — Éléments de démographie*, Paris, Presses Universitaires de France, 1976.

Savory, (T.H.), *British spiders: their haunts and habits*, Oxford, Clarendon Press, 1926.

Schneider (Anna), *Fleurs de sang, 61 poèmes à dire*, Lille, Imprimeries de Desclée, de Brower et Co, 1923.

Seabury (Paul), *The rise and decline of the cold war*, New York, Basic Books, 1967.

Segond (Joseph), *La Guerre mondiale et la vie spirituelle*, Paris, Félix Alcan, 1918.

Seignolle (Claude), *Le Folklore de la Provence*, Paris, G.P. Maisonneuve et Larose, 1967.

Senescau (L.D. de), *Surmufles et bourreaux: le Kaiser, la kultur, les Boches, et leurs amis*, Bordeaux, Imprimerie de Gounouilhou, 1916.

Serouya (Henri), *Le Problème philosophique de la guerre et de la paix*, Paris, Marcel Rivière, 1932.

Serre (Joseph), *Deuils et gloires*, Chants patriotiques, Lyon, E. Vitte, 1916.

Sertillanges (père A.D.), *Bréviaire du combattant*, Paris, Flammarion, 1940.

Servan (admiral Victor), *Aux combattants et aux morts pour la patrie*, Montpellier, Imprimerie de la Manufacture de la Charité, 1914.

SIPRI (Stockholm International Peace Research Institute) *Outer space*

— *battlefield of the future?*, London, Taylor and Francis, 1978. — *Weapons of mass destruction and the environment*, London, Taylor and Francis, 1977. — *World armaments and disarmament* (SIPRI) year book, 1985), London, Taylor and Francis, 1985.

Sorel (Georges-Eugène), *Réflexions sur la violence*, Paris, Librairies de "Pages Libres", 1908.

Sorrell (Vernon G.), *War and society, Proceedings of the Institute of World Affairs. 18th session*, University of Southern California, 1940.

Spade (Henri), *Et pourquoi pas la patrie?*, Paris, Juillard, 1974.

Spencer (Herbert), *De l'éducation*, Paris, G. Baillière, 1880. — *Principes de sociologie*, traduit de l'anglais par M.E. Cazelles, Paris, G. Baillière (4 vol.), 1878-1883.

Spont (Henry), *Psychologie de la guerre*, Paris, Perrin, 1920.

Steinmetz (Sebald Rudolf), *Der Krieg als sociologisches Problem*, Amsterdam, Wersluys, 1899. Voir Constantin, *Le rôle sociologique de la guerre et le sentiment national.* — *Die Philosophie des Krieges*, Leipzig, J.A. Barth, 1907.

Stirner (Max) pseudonym of Schmidt (Johann Caspar), *L'Unique et sa propriété*, traduction et préface de Henri Lasvignes, Paris, éditions de la "Revue blanche", 1900.

Strautz (von), *Irh wollt Elsass und Lothringen une mehr . . .*, paru en 1887, réédité à Berlin, Librairie politique, 1912.

Tavernier (Jean-Baptiste), *Les Six Voyages de Jean-Baptiste Tavernier, etc.*, tome V, Relations du Japon et du Tonkin, Paris, G. Clouzier, 1679-1682.

"Techniques nées de la guerre", revue *Réalités,* no 1, février 1946.

Temple (William), *A conditional justification of war*, London, Hodder & Stoughton 1940. — Why does God allow war? London, S.P.C.K., 1941.

Teppe (Julien), *L'Idole Patrie*, Paris, éditions du Centre, 1967.

Thellier de Poncheville (chanoine Charles), *Dieu et la guerre*, Paris, Bonne Presse, 1939. — *Notre petite sœur Thérèse et nous en guerre*, Paris, éditions Alsatia, 1940.

Théry (Edmond-Amédée), *Conséquences économiques de la guerre (de 14) pour la France*, Paris, Berlin frères, 1922.

Thiéry (Henri), *Glanes de guerre*, Paris, H. Baragon, 1916.

Thuriet (Charles Émilien), *Traditions populaires de la Haute-Saône et du Jura*, Paris, E. Lechevalier, 1892.

Tolstoï (Alexis), *Écrits sur la guerre* (from the Russian), Paris, Nagel, 1945.

Toulat (Jean), *La Bombe ou la vie*, Paris, Fayard, 1969.

Toulat (Pierre), *Des Évêques face au problème des armes*, Paris, Le Centurion, 1973.

Triac (Jean de), *Guerre et christianisme*, Paris, Firmin-Didot, 1896.

Trolard (Eugène), *Pèlerinage aux champs de bataille français d'Italie. I De*

Montenotte au Pont d'Arcole. II. De Rivoli à Marengo et à Solferino, Paris, A. Savine, 1893.

Truppenführung, Code of Conduct for German troops, Paris, Berger-Levrault, 1936.

Tzschirner (Heinrich Gottlieb), *Ueber den Krieg; en philosophischer Versuch*, Leipzig, Barth, 1815.

Ullrich (J.), *La Guerre à travers les âges*. Translated by H.J. Ferget, Paris, Gallimard, 1942.

Vaccaro (Michele Angelo), *La lotta per l'esistanza e suoi effeti sull' umanita*, Roma, 1886.

Vacher de Lapouge (Georges), *Les Sélections sociales*, cours libre de sciences politiques professé à l'université de Montpellier (1888–1889), Paris, A. Fontemoing, 1896.

Les valeurs fondamentales du patriotisme français (notice rédigée par une commission interarmées), Paris, Addim, 1962.

Van der Verren (Auguste), *France! Hommage au peuple souverain, etc.* Paris, 2 rue Titon, 1915.

Vanel (A.H.), *Fleurs sanglantes, poésies*, Delle, Imprimerie de V. Petitjean, 1916.

Vassivière (Pierre-Joseph de Vassivière, dit Joseph), *L'Ame française, ode à la France*, Paris, A. Lemerre, 1918.

Verdier (cardinal Jean), *Le Cardinal parle à la France*, Paris éditions Alsatia, 1940. — *Consignes du temps de guerre*, Paris, Flammarion, 1940.

Vermeil (Édouard), *Doctrinaires de la révolution allemande (1918–1938)*, Paris, F. Sorlot, 1938. — *Le Racisme allemand, essai de mise au point*, Paris, F. Sorlot, 1939.

Vernier-Baduel (Marie), *Bouquet de France, 1914–1917, tableaux et scènes de guerre*, Montpellier, Imprimeries de Firmin et Montane, 1918.

Veuillot (Louis), *La Guerre et l'homme de guerre*, Paris, L. Vivès, 1855.

Vézère (Jean), pseudonym de Vergniaud (Suzanne), *Chants des enfants de France: cantiques, rondes et chansons*, Paris, Maison de la Bonne Presse, 1915.

Vignes Rouges (Jean des), pseudonyme de Taboureau (colonel Jean), *L'Ame des chefs, récits de guerre et méditations*, Paris, Perrin, 1917.

Vignol (capitaine René), *Définition de l'aggresseur dans la guerre*, Paris, Librairie du Recueil Sirey, 1933.

Villeneuve (Roland), *Le Musée des supplices*, Paris, éditions Azur, 1968.

War and society, Proceedings of the Institute of World Affairs, Los Angeles, 1941.

War letters of fallen Englishmen, edited by Laurence Housman, London, Victor Gollancz, 1930.

Werner (général Major), *La Grande Peur, la troisième guerre mondiale?*, Bruxelles, éditions Rossel, 1976.

Wet (général Rudolf de), *Trois Ans de guerre* (Sur la guerre des Boers), Paris, F. Juven, 1902.

Wheeler (W.M.), *The social insects*, London; Kegan Paul, 1928. — *Social life among the insects*, London, Constable and Co, 1923.

Willaert (Père Léopold, S.J.), *Religion et patriotisme*, Paris, Casterman, 1947.

Wolker (Dr Gertrud), *Der Kommende Giftgaskrieg* Leipzig, 1925.

World Military and Social Expendtures, edited by Ruth Leger Sivard, Leesburg (Virginia, U.S.A.), WMSE Publications, 1978 et 1980.

Wormser-Migot (Olga), *Le Système concentrationnaire nazi, 1933-1945*, Paris, Presses Universitaires de France, 1968.

Wright (Quincy), *A study of war*, Chicago, University of Chicago Press, 1942.

Wulf (Maurice de), *Guerre et philosophie*, Paris, Bloud et Gay, 1915.

Ysiad, *L'Allemagne et son enfant terrible, Maximilien Harden*, Paris, Berger-Levrault, 1918.

Zuckerman (S.), *The social life of monkeys and apes*, London, Kegan Paul, 1931.

Index